A~Z
OF
BEAD
EMBROIDERY

I'll give my jewels for a set of beads,
My gorgeous palace for a hermitage…

WILLIAM SHAKESPEARE

• • •

- CONTENTS -

*"Life is a train of moods like a string of beads; and as we pass through them
they prove to be many colored lenses, which paint the world their own hue,
and each shows us only what lies in its own focus."*

RALPH WALDO EMERSON

Contents

Editor and Author
Sue Gardner

Editorial team
Lizzie Kulinski, Marian Carpenter

Patterns and Illustrations
Kathleen Barac

Design and Layout
Lynton Grandison

Photography
Andrew Dunbar

Publisher
Margie Bauer

Distribution enquiries
Country Bumpkin Publications
315 Unley Road, Malvern
South Australia 5061 Australia
Phone: 08 8372 7600
Fax: 08 8372 7601
Email: marketing@countrybumpkin.com.au
Website: www.countrybumpkin.com.au

PUBLISHED IN AUSTRALIA
Printed and bound in China

A - Z of Bead Embroidery

ISBN 0-9750920-7-3

- BEADS -

Beads

TYPES OF BEADS

Throughout history, beads have been made from a vast range of materials and in an enormous variety of shapes and sizes. Shells, stones, seeds, wood, bones, minerals, metals and clays have all been used for making beads.

BEADED FIRESCREEN, ENGLISH MID 19C

The designs in this book feature the following beads:

Seed beads, also known as rocailles, are round donut-shaped glass beads.

Pony beads are large seed beads, generally in sizes 5, 6 and 8.

Petite beads are small seed beads, generally in sizes 14 and 15.

Hex cut beads are made from a six-sided glass cane that is cut into short lengths. They look like very short bugle beads.

Cylinder beads are small tubular beads that generally have a large hole. Delicas, Magnificas and Antiques are all types of cylinder beads.

Bugle beads are made from glass canes that are cut into lengths varying from 2 - 30mm (1/16 - 1 1/8").

Sequins are usually discs made from metal or plastic. They can be flat or cupped and are also known as paillettes.

Faceted beads are made from cut glass or lead crystal and come in a variety of shapes and sizes.

Pearls, both natural and artificial, are available in various sizes.

Diamantes are technically not beads as they do not have a hole. These are held in a claw clasp or bead cap that is attached to the fabric. They are also known as rhinestones.

Gemstone chips are small irregularly shaped pieces of gemstones that have usually been tumbled.

Moulded beads are made from glass or plastic and are produced in a wide variety of shapes. Flower beads fall in this category.

GLASS BEAD FINISHES

Transparent beads are made from clear or coloured glass that allows light to readily pass through it.

Translucent beads allow some light to pass through them, but not as much as transparent beads. They can also be known as greasy, satin or opal.

Opaque beads consist of solid coloured glass that does not permit any light through it.

Lustre beads have a subtle sheen, which is the result of a transparent coating.

Frosted beads are transparent or translucent beads that have been dipped or tumbled in acid.

Gloss beads are particularly shiny.

Matte beads have a dull surface. They are made from opaque

beads that have been dipped or tumbled in acid.

Metallic beads are those beads that have been painted or treated in some way to create a metallic appearance.

Colourlined beads are clear or coloured beads with the hole lined with another colour.

Silverlined beads are similar to a colourlined bead but the hole is lined with silver. These beads have a lot of sparkle.

AB stands for aurora borealis. They are made from dark opaque beads that are treated with metal salts. Also known as iris or rainbow beads.

SIZES OF BEADS

Beads come in an enormous range of sizes. For many, their size is indicated by the measurement across the width of the bead in millimetres.

Numbers are used to indicate the sizes of beads such as Delica and seed beads - the higher the number the smaller the bead.

Size 11 beads are the most commonly used beads.

Size 14 and 15 beads are also known as petite beads.

Size 5, 6 and 8 beads are also called pony beads.

Other materials

FABRICS

Almost any fabric, from sheer organzas to heavy furnishing fabrics, can be used for beading. The fabric must pass two criteria - it must be strong enough to support the weight of the beads you are applying and you must be able to pass a needle through it. The weave needs to be firm enough so the beads do not slip through to the wrong side.

Interfacing can be added to your fabric to provide a firmer surface for stitching on as well as adding strength to the fabric. Sheer fabrics can be backed with netting to give additional support.

THREADS

Use a fine thread as this will be easier to thread into the type of needle necessary for beading. The colour of the thread is usually matched to the background fabric but interesting effects can also be achieved with contrasting threads.

Nymo is a specialist beading thread made from waxed nylon. It is available in a variety of sizes but size D is the most commonly used. Before using Nymo thread, gently pull a small section at a time along the entire length. This pre-stretching removes twists and helps to prevent pulls after the beading is worked.

Silk thread is also suitable for beading. It is a very strong, pliable thread and like machine sewing threads, it is available in an enormous range of colours.

Synthetic machine sewing threads are a useful alternative for bead embroidery. These threads are both strong and fine. Pass the thread through some beeswax to make it more manageable.

Tools and equipment

NEEDLES

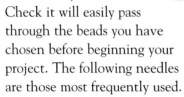

Always use a needle with a slender shaft and small eye. Check it will easily pass through the beads you have chosen before beginning your project. The following needles are those most frequently used.

Beading needles are longer than most other types of needles and have a flat eye. Sizes 10 and 13 are the most commonly used. They do bend and can break easily.

Straw (milliner's) needles also have a longer shaft than most needles and the small eye is only marginally wider than the shaft.

Sharp needles are sharp and slender with a small round eye. This provides strength for the needle and reduces wear on the thread.

If you are having difficulty taking the needle through a bead, don't force it as you may crack the bead. Change to a smaller needle or discard the bead.

HOOPS AND FRAMES

A hoop or frame is an invaluable tool for beading. It allows you to place your stitches more accurately and helps to prevent the stitching from puckering the fabric. Ensure the entire design fits within the hoop or frame.

Hoops

Hoops can be hand held, free standing, or able to be attached to a table with a clamp. Those that can be tightened with a screwdriver will hold the fabric more firmly than spring hoops. Binding the inner ring of a hoop also aids in achieving a firm tension on the fabric. It is also kinder on your fabric than an unbound hoop. Wooden hoops tend to grip the fabric much better than metal or plastic ones.

Hand held hoops are wonderful for small projects. The down side is that one hand must always be used to hold the hoop. Free standing and clamp hoops have the added advantage of leaving both your hands free to handle the needle and thread. Tambour work needs a free standing or clamp hoop.

- TOOLS AND EQUIPMENT -

Once your fabric is held firmly in a hoop or frame, avoid pressing on it with your fingers, as this will alter the tension. Constantly check the firmness of the fabric and adjust as often as necessary to ensure you are always stitching on a taut surface. Remember to always remove the fabric from the hoop when you are not working on it. This helps to prevent the hoop from permanently marking the fabric.

Frames

A frame always needs to be wider than the piece of fabric required for the design. If using a slat frame, this applies to the height as well. A roller frame will allow you to scroll down the fabric as your design progresses. However, this can be a time consuming process as the sides will require relacing each time you reposition the length of fabric.

If your frame is much larger than the piece of fabric you wish to work on, attach panels of a similar weight fabric to the sides before mounting it in the frame. Alternatively, use a backing fabric that is an appropriate size for the frame. Baste your selected fabric to the centre of the backing fabric and stitch through both layers.

Many frames come with adjustable stands so you can alter the angle and height of the taut fabric to suit your comfort and stitching requirements. Like free standing and clamp hoops, these enable you to devote both hands to the task of stitching and handling the thread.

NEEDLE THREADERS AND GRABBERS

Needle threaders

If you are having difficulty threading your needle, a needle threader may help. Push the threader's wire loop through the eye of the needle and then take the thread through the wire loop. Pull the needle off the loop, leaving the thread through the needle.

Needle grabbers

Use a piece of fine rubber, or even a small square from a balloon, to grip the needle when pulling it through beads with several threads through them.

STORAGE CONTAINERS

Store your beads in small, lidded glass or plastic containers away from direct sunlight. Specialist beading shops offer a variety of storage systems. Those small plastic containers that rolls of film come in make excellent containers as do the multi-drawer cabinets that hardware shops sell for nails and screws. Fishing tackle boxes are another suitable alternative.

Re-using Tic Tac flip top boxes are excellent for very tiny beads. The box is great for pouring out beads and when you want to return beads to the box, just pull off the whole top and return the unused beads.

Round stackable containers are another excellent way of storing beads. They are relatively inexpensive and come in a variety of sizes but as there is only one lid for the top section, care must be taken when removing each section, or the beads may escape.

- TOOLS AND EQUIPMENT -

Plastic zip lock bags are also suitable as they are light and pliable. They are particularly good for storing beads such as those made from sterling silver as they keep the air from tarnishing the silver.

Divided boxes with only a single lid are best used for larger beads that can easily be handled, rather than tiny beads.

Small dishes are useful for holding the beads you are currently using. Condiment dishes are excellent for this. Special bead trays can be purchased from beading shops. Have several dishes available so you don't have to mix the different bead colours and types.

BEAD MATS

A bead mat will allow you to spread out a selection of the beads you are using. This enables you to easily inspect the beads and discard any you do not wish to use.

A square of felt, velvet or suede works well as the beads do not roll away.

WAXES AND CONDITIONERS

Conditioning the thread will help to eliminate tangling and make it easier to handle. Beeswax is a traditional conditioner but a cake of bath soap or paraffin wax can also be used. Today there are also commercially available thread conditioners. These can often be found in specialist beading or embroidery supply shops.

To add beeswax or soap to a length of thread, draw the thread across the surface of the beeswax or soap while keeping it taut. Hold the thread up with one hand and run the fingernails of your other hand down the thread to remove excess wax or soap.

SCISSORS

Good quality, well maintained scissors make a huge difference to the ease and quality of your work. Two pairs of scissors are recommended - a small pair with fine, sharp blades and tip for snipping threads and a larger, heavier pair for cutting fabric.

To maintain your scissors, never use them for anything but their intended purpose. Even cutting paper or trimming your fingernails with them will blunt the blades prematurely.

The most common cause of damage to scissors is dropping them and have them land on their points. To reduce this risk, make a small, weighted scissor pillow and attach it to the handle. This way they will be less likely to land on their points. Your scissors will also benefit from applying a small drop of oil to the screw on a regular basis. Baby oil or sewing machine oil is suitable.

PLIERS

Small needle nose pliers are a handy addition to your beading tool kit. Use them to carefully crush strung beads that are incorrectly positioned.

FRENCH BEADWORK PURSE, LATE 18C

- T R A N S F E R R I N G   D E S I G N S -

Transferring designs

There are a variety of methods and tools available to help you transfer your chosen design from paper to fabric. The method you choose will depend on personal preference, the size and intricacy of the design, your choice of fabric and the use of the finished piece.

Iron-on transfers

Commercially made transfers are very quick and easy to use. They do leave permanent marks so you must ensure your stitching will completely cover the design lines. To obtain a clear imprint you need to choose a smooth fabric.

Many transfers are accompanied with clear instructions from the manufacturer, but if they don't, the following method will work successfully with most iron-on transfers.

Cover a smooth flat surface such as a wooden board with aluminium foil, shiny side up. Place the fabric over the board right side up. Position the transfer, face down, onto the fabric and pin in place. Using a medium to hot iron and a press and lift action, press firmly for a few seconds. Never glide the iron over the transfer as this can smudge the ink and move the transfer. Carefully lift a corner of the transfer to check that the design has transferred clearly. If not, continue pressing until the design lines are clearly visible. Take care not to scorch the fabric and if necessary use a lightweight pressing cloth to help prevent this from happening.

Heat sensitive transfer pencils work in the same way as the commercially produced iron-on transfers but give you a much wider scope for your design. Draw or trace a mirror image of the design onto tracing paper. Transfer the design to the fabric following the procedure above.

Direct tracing

With this method the more transparent the fabric the easier it is to see the design. Placing a light source behind the fabric will make it appear more transparent. Use a light box or tape the design to a sun-filled window.

Draw or trace your design onto tracing paper with black ink or a black felt tipped pen. Tape the tracing to a flat surface (this could be your window or light box). Position the fabric over the tracing and tape in place. Trace over the design lines with a lead pencil, fabric marking pen, or chalk-based marker.

Templates

Templates are useful for transferring simple shapes that are to be repeated several times. Draw or trace the required shape onto heavy paper, cardboard or plastic and cut out. Position the template on the right side of the fabric and trace around it with a pencil or fabric marker.

Alternatively, trace the shape onto tracing or baking paper and cut out. Position the shape onto the right side of the fabric and pin in place. Using contrasting thread, tack around the shape very close to the edge.

- TRANSFERRING DESIGNS -

Almost any object can be used as a template. Coins, cups, bottles and plates are useful for creating circles. Small boxes and books, plastic stencils, biscuit cutters and French curves provide a large range of re-usable shapes.

'REJOICE' BY CAROLYN PEARCE
INSPIRATIONS 47

Tacking

This is a very time consuming method but it leaves no permanent marks on the fabric.

Trace the design onto tracing or tissue paper. Position the tracing onto the right side of the fabric and pin in place. Using a thread that contrasts with the fabric colour, tack along the design lines with small even running stitches. Score the tacked lines with the tip of the needle and tear the paper away. With tissue paper, you can wipe over the design lines with a damp sponge and then tear the paper away.

Transfer papers

Dressmaker's carbon is suitable for fabrics with a smooth surface and is produced in several colours, so choose a colour that contrasts with your fabric colour. Like iron-on transfers, the markings are permanent.

Spread the fabric out flat, right side up, on a smooth hard surface. Tape in place. Place the carbon onto the fabric, waxed side down. Position the drawing of the design over the carbon and tape in place. Trace over the design lines with a sharp pencil, ballpoint pen or tracing wheel.

Wax free transfer paper is available in several different colours and is used in exactly the same way as dressmaker's carbon. As it can be erased like pencil or rinsed out, it is a very satis-factory method when working with smooth fabrics.

HE WOULD TELL OF THE
WHORL OF LIGHT
THAT WAS INFINITY TO BE SEEN
IN GLASS, OR A SHELL,
OR A BEAD, OR A PEARL.

HILDA DOOLITTLE

- *Attaching a single seed or cylinder bead - Method 1 (whip stitch)* -

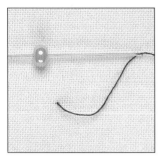

1. Secure the thread on the back of the fabric and bring it to the front. Thread the bead onto the needle.

2. Slide the bead down the thread to the fabric.

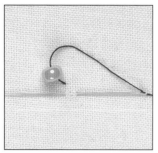

3. At the base of the bead, make a stitch the same length as the width of the bead, from right to left, through the fabric.

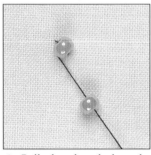

4. Pull the thread through. Thread a second bead onto the needle and slide it down the thread to the fabric.

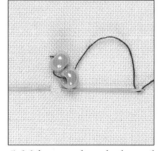

5. Make a stitch at the base of the bead in the same manner as before.

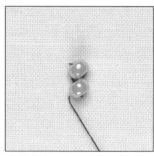

6. Pull the thread through.

7. Continue attaching beads in the same manner.

8. After threading the last bead, take the needle through the fabric as before but do not re-emerge.

9. Pull the thread through and end off on the back of fabric.

EARLY HISTORY

The use of shells, bone, seeds, pebbles and wood were probably the beginnings of decorative beadwork. They were frequently used to make amulets to protect the wearer from coming to any harm.

Traditionally, children in western society wore coral necklaces to keep them safe from illness or evil.

Beads were also a valuable source of barter and currency. Many types of materials have been used to make beads including porcelain, turquoise and clay. In ancient Egypt, lapis lazuli was used and the ancient Greeks used granulated gold.

Stone Age grave sites in Israel have revealed traces of head dresses that are elaborately embroidered with beads made from broken bones and shells from the Mediterranean Sea. Flat disc shaped beads of shell, stone and pottery have been found in Egyptian sarcophagi.

Glass, however became the most widely used material.

- Method 2 (back stitch) -

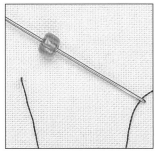 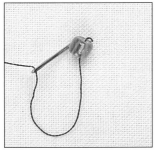

1. Secure the thread on the back of the fabric and bring it to the front. Thread the bead onto the needle.

2. Slide the bead down the thread to the fabric. Take the needle to the back at the end of the bead.

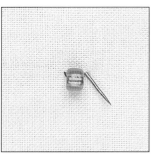 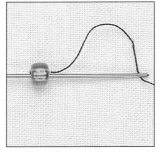

3. Pull the thread through. Re-emerge at the other end of the bead.

4. Take the needle through the bead again.

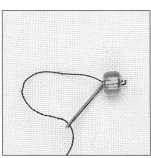 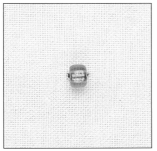

5. Pull the thread through. Take the needle to the back of the fabric at the end of the bead.

6. Pull the thread through. End off on the back of the fabric.

- Method 3 (hole at the top) -

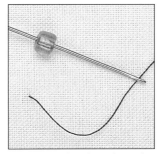 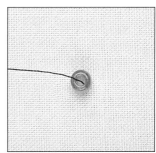

1. Secure the thread on the back of the fabric and bring it to the front. Thread the bead onto the needle.

2. Slide the bead down the thread to the fabric. Hold the bead on the fabric so the hole is uppermost.

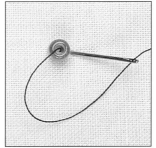 

3. Take the needle to the back of the fabric on one side of the bead.

4. Pull the thread through. Bring the needle up through the bead again.

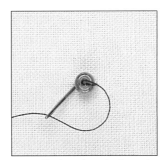 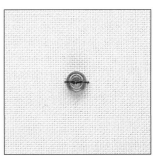

5. Pull the thread through. Take the needle to the back of the fabric on the other side of the bead.

6. Pull the thread through. End off on the back of the fabric.

- Attaching a pair of beads -

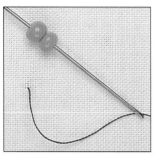

1. Secure the thread on the back of the fabric and bring it to the front. Thread two beads onto the needle.

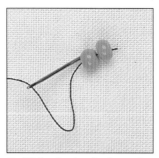

2. Slide the beads down the thread to the fabric. Take the needle to the back at the end of the second bead.

3. Pull the thread through. Re-emerge at the end of the first bead.

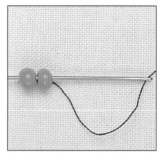

4. Take the needle through both beads again.

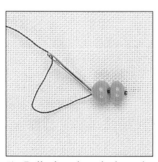

5. Pull the thread through. Take the needle to the back of the fabric at the end of the second bead.

6. Pull the thread through. Bring the needle to the front between the two beads.

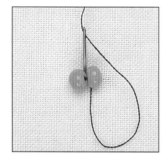

7. Pull the thread through. Take the needle to the back of the fabric just over the threads between the beads.

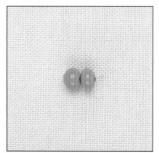

8. Pull the thread through. Secure the thread on the back of the fabric.

GLASS BEADS

The Venetian glass industry began during the 11th century and was established on the island of Murano, where it remains today. The glass workers were put onto the island because of the fire risk to the city.

As glass bead making spread from Venice to Bohemia and across northern Europe, the techniques of using them in embroidery spread to private homes and convents.

MURANO BEADS

In 1549, the first glass manufacturing houses were established in London, and Amsterdam had a glass industry from 1608 to 1680. It supplied the needs of the Dutch East India Company as a trading commodity.

Czechoslovakia's glass bead industry was centred around the town of Jablonec. Much of the work was done by men from nearby prisons and each prisoner was expected to make approximately ten thousand beads per day.

Today Japan is one of the leading producers of fine glass beads.

- *Attaching multiple beads* - Method 1 (*whip stitch*) -

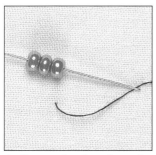

1. Secure the thread on the back of the fabric and bring it to the front. Thread three beads onto the needle.

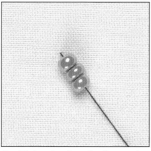

2. Slide the beads down the thread to the fabric.

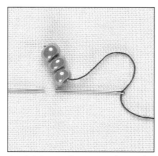

3. Make a horizontal stitch, the same length as the width of one bead, from right to left through the fabric at the base of the last bead.

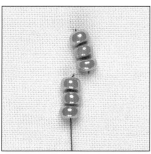

4. Pull the thread through. Thread a second group of three beads onto the needle and slide them down the thread to the fabric.

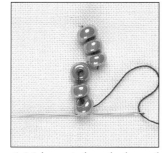

5. Make a stitch at the base of the last bead in the same manner as before.

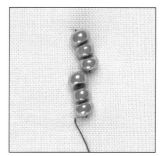

6. Pull the thread through.

7. Continue attaching groups of three beads in the same manner.

8. After threading the last bead, take the needle through the fabric as before but do not re-emerge.

9. Pull the thread through and end off on the back of the fabric.

HINTS ON THREADING A NEEDLE

If you have difficulty threading a needle try one of the following -

Take the needle to the thread, rather than the thread to the needle.

Wear some waxy lip balm. When you moisten the end of the thread, it will be coated with the wax and this will help prevent the end from splitting.

Use a needle with a larger eye, but check that it will still pass through your beads.

- *Method 2 (back stitch through each bead)* -

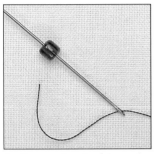

1. Secure the thread on the back of the fabric and bring it to the front. Thread a bead onto the needle.

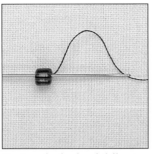

2. Attach the bead following steps 2 - 4 of method 2 on page 15.

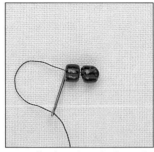

3. Pull the thread through. Thread a second bead onto the needle. Take the needle to the back of the fabric at the end of the bead.

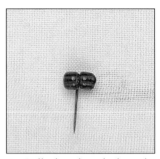

4. Pull the thread through. Re-emerge between the two beads.

5. Take the needle through the second bead again.

6. Pull the thread through. Thread a third bead onto the needle.

7. Secure the bead to the fabric in the same manner as before.

8. Continue attaching the required number of beads in the same manner. After attaching the last bead, take the thread to the back of the fabric and secure.

BEADS AND NATIVE AMERICANS

During the early part of the 17th century, glass bead production found it's way to the new colony of Jamestown, Virginia in the US. There, the Venetian craftsmen made pea-sized beads and used them for trading with the local Indians.

Prior to the arrival of the settlers, native American Indians were already using beads made from clay and shell but were immediately taken with these new colourful glass beads.

The natives used a bow loom to weave belts and sashes, which were often entirely of beads. They also strung the beads and interwove the string at intervals to make patterns on the surface of woven fabric.

Embroidery with glass beads became popular and gradually replaced the old methods of working with moose hair and porcupine quills. Glass beads began to decorate moccasins, waistcoats and head bands. This type of embroidery was influenced by the French and Spanish nuns in the missionary schools and convents, who used a combination of traditional geometric patterns and European floral designs.

TOBACCO BAG, 1890

- Method 3 (back stitch through selected beads) -

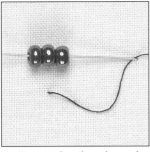

1. Secure the thread on the back of the fabric and bring it to the front. Thread three beads onto the needle.

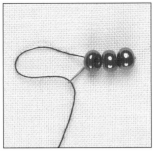

2. Slide the beads down the thread to the fabric. Take the needle to the back at the end of the last bead.

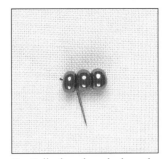

3. Pull the thread through. Re-emerge between the last two beads.

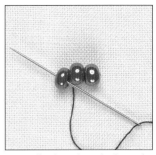

4. Pull the thread through. Take the needle through the last bead again.

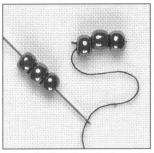

5. Pull the thread through. Thread a further three beads onto the needle.

6. Slide the beads down the thread to the fabric. Take the needle to the back at the end of the last bead.

7. Pull the thread through. Re-emerge between the last two beads.

8. Pull the thread through. Take the needle through the last bead again.

9. Following steps 5 - 8, continue attaching the required number of beads in the same manner.

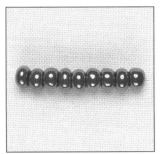

10. After attaching the last bead, take the thread to the back of the fabric and secure.

'SAFE KEEPING' BY JANE NICHOLAS, INSPIRATIONS 34

- Method 4 (couching using two needles) -

1. Secure the thread on the back of the fabric and bring it to the front. Thread the required number of beads onto the needle and thread.

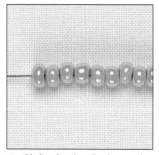

2. Slide the beads down the thread, laying them on the fabric.

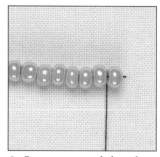

3. Secure a second thread on the back of the fabric and bring it to the front between the first and second beads.

4. Take the needle to the back of the fabric just over the thread between the two beads.

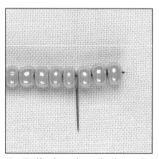

5. Pull the thread through. Re-emerge between the third and fourth beads.

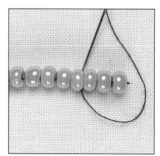

6. Pull the thread through. Take the needle to the back of the fabric just over the thread between the two beads.

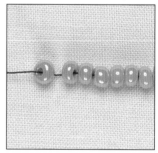

7. Pull the thread through. Continue couching the thread after every third bead in the same manner.

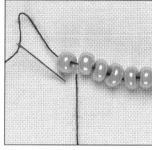

8. When almost at the end of the line of beads, take the thread that is threaded through the beads to the back of the fabric.

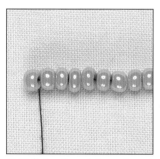

9. Pull the thread through and end off on the back of the fabric.

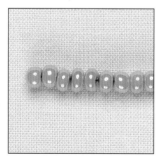

10. After the last couching stitch, secure this thread on the back of the fabric as well.

'BERRY DELIGHT' BY JAN KERTON, INSPIRATIONS 37

- Method 5 (couching) -

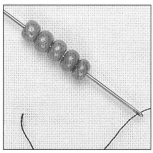 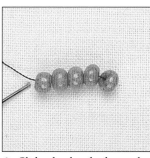 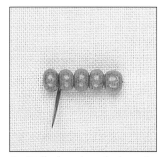 

1. Secure the thread on the back of the fabric and bring it to the front. Thread the required number of beads onto the needle.

2. Slide the beads down the thread. Take the needle to the back of the fabric at the required position.

3. Pull the thread through. Bring the needle to the front between the last two beads.

4. Pull the thread through. Take the needle to the back of the fabric just over the thread between the two beads.

 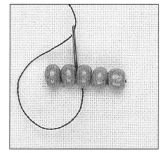  

5. Pull the thread through. Re-emerge between the next two beads.

6. Pull the thread through. Take it to the back of the fabric just over the thread between the two beads.

7. Pull the thread through. Continue couching the thread between the beads in the same manner.

8. To finish, secure the thread on the back of the fabric after the last couching stitch.

- Method 6 (lazy squaw stitch) -

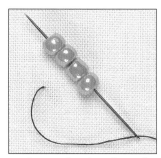 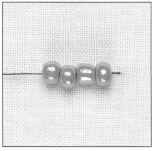  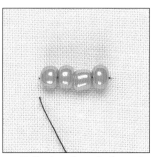

1. Secure the thread on the back of the fabric and bring it to the front. Thread onto the needle the number of beads required for one row.

2. Slide the beads down the thread to the fabric.

3. Take the needle to the back of the fabric at the end of the last bead.

4. Pull the thread through. Bring the thread to the front at the starting point for the second row (a bead's width below where it went to the back).

- Method 6 - lazy squaw stitch - continued

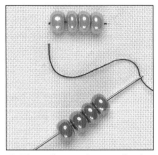

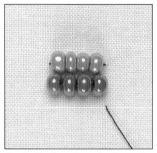

5. Thread onto the needle the number of beads required for the second row.

6. Slide the beads down the thread to the fabric. Take the needle to the back of the fabric at the end of the last bead.

7. Pull the thread through. Bring the thread to the front at the starting point for the third row (a bead's width below where it went to the back).

8. Continue attaching rows of beads in the same manner. End off on the back of the fabric after the last row.

- Method 7 - lazy stitch -

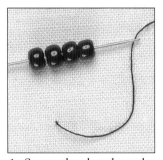

1. Secure the thread on the back of the fabric and bring it to the front. Thread up to seven beads onto the needle.

2. Slide the beads down thread, laying them on the fabric.

3. Take the needle to the back of the fabric at the end of the last bead.

4. Pull the thread through. Bring the needle to the front a short distance away, making a tiny stitch.

5. Pull the thread through. Thread a second group of beads onto the needle.

6. Slide the beads down the thread and take the needle to the back of the fabric at the end of the last bead as before.

7. Pull the thread through. Bring the thread to the front a short distance away.

8. Continue attaching groups of beads in the same manner. End off on the back of the fabric after the last group of beads.

- Attaching a single bugle bead - Method 1 (whip stitch)

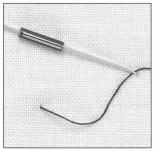

1. Secure the thread on the back of the fabric and bring it to the front. Thread the bead onto the needle.

2. Slide the bead down the thread to the fabric.

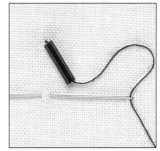

3. Make a horizontal stitch, the same length as the width of the bead, from right to left through the fabric at the base of the bead.

4. Pull the thread through. Thread a second bead onto the needle and slide it down the thread to the fabric.

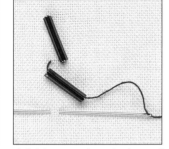

5. Make a stitch at the base of the bead in the same manner as before.

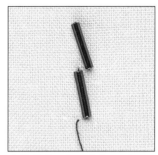

6. Pull the thread through.

7. Continue attaching beads in the same manner.

8. After threading the last bead, take the needle through the fabric as before but do not re-emerge.

9. Pull the thread through and end off on the back of the fabric.

BUGLE BEADS

Bugle beads can be smooth and round or faceted. Some Indian bugle beads are twisted and elaborately painted.

During the nineteenth century, bugle beads were very popular for decorating household items and accessories. In the 'flapper' period of the early twentieth century, they were used extensively on dresses. Some dresses had as much as 4kg (9lbs) of additional weight due to the beading that embellished them.

Always wax or condition your thread when stitching bugle beads as their cut ends are more abrasive on the thread than the ends of most other beads.

Discard any beads that are chipped or broken as they will cut the thread.

To attach a bugle bead so it stands away from the fabric, thread a small bead onto the needle after the bugle bead. Take the thread back through the bugle bead only.

- *Method 2 (back stitch)* -

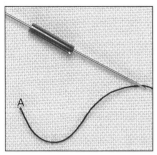

1. Secure the thread on the back of the fabric and bring it to the front (A). Thread the bead onto the needle.

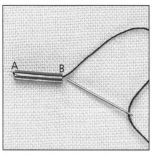

2. Slide the bead down the thread to the fabric. Take the needle to the back at the end of the bead (B).

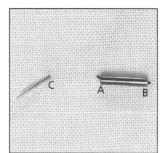

3. Pull the thread through. Re-emerge at C, a bead's length away from A.

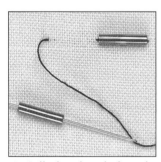

4. Pull the thread through. Thread a second bead onto the needle.

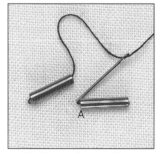

5. Pull the thread through. Take the needle to the back of the fabric at A.

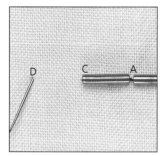

6. Pull the thread through. Re-emerge at D, a bead's length away from C.

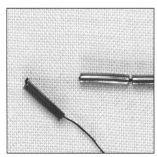

7. Continue attaching beads in the same manner.

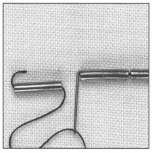

8. After threading the last bead, take the needle through the fabric between the last two beads.

9. Pull the thread through and end off on the back of the fabric.

BIRTHSTONES

JANUARY
Garnet

FEBRUARY
Amethyst

MARCH
Bloodstone or Aquamarine

APRIL
Diamond

MAY
Emerald

JUNE
Pearl or Moonstone

JULY
Ruby

AUGUST
Sardonyx or Peridot

SEPTEMBER
Sapphire

OCTOBER
Opal or Tourmaline

NOVEMBER
Topaz

DECEMBER
Turquoise or Lapiz lazuli

- Method 3 (detached chain) -

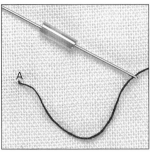

1. Secure the thread on the back of the fabric and bring it to the front at A. Thread the bead onto the needle.

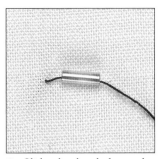

2. Slide the bead down the thread to the fabric.

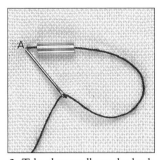

3. Take the needle to the back at A.

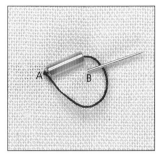

4. Begin to pull the thread through. Re-emerge at B, taking the needle between the end of the bead and the loop of thread. The distance from A - B is the same as the length of the bead.

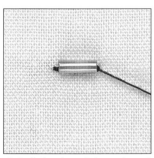

5. Pull the thread through and settle the bead in place.

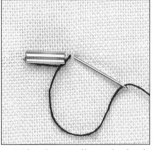

6. Take the needle to the back of the fabric just over the loop of thread.

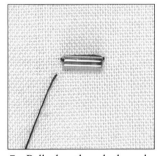

7. Pull the thread through. Bring the thread to the front at the position for the second bead.

8. Attach in the same manner as before. Continue attaching the required number of beads. After attaching the last bead, end off on the back of the fabric.

Alternative method

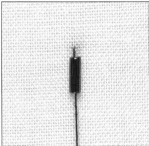

1. Repeat steps 1 - 2 above.

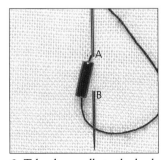

2. Take the needle to the back at A and re-emerge at B, inside the loop of thread. The distance from A - B is the same as the length of the bead.

3. Pull the thread through and tighten the loop.

4. Take the needle to the back of the fabric just over the loop. Pull the thread through. End off on the back of the fabric.

- Bead loops -

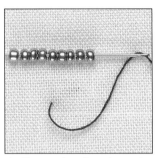   

1. Secure the thread on the back of the fabric and bring it to the front. Thread the required number of beads onto the needle.

2. Slide the beads down the thread to the fabric. Take the needle to the back of the fabric a short distance away from where it emerged.

3. Pull the thread through. Secure the thread with 1 - 2 tiny back stitches.

4. Work the required number of bead loops in the same manner. End off on the back of the fabric.

- Circle of beads -

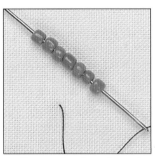  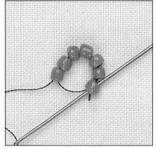 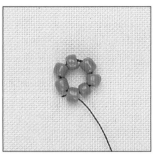

1. Secure the thread on the back of the fabric and bring it to the front. Thread the required number of beads onto the needle.

2. Pull the thread through. Take the needle through all beads in the same order that they were first threaded onto the needle.

3. Pull the thread through. Take the needle through the first bead.

4. Pull the thread firmly to pull the beads into a circle.

   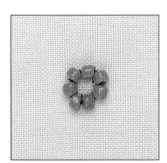

5. Position the circle on the fabric. Take the needle to the back of the fabric between the first and second beads.

6. Pull the thread through. Re-emerge between the second and third beads.

7. Couch the beads to the fabric following steps 4 - 7 on page 21.

8. To finish, secure the thread on the back of the fabric after the last couching stitch.

- Attaching a bead to the end of a bead -

 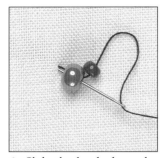  

1. Secure the thread on the back of the fabric and bring it to the front. Thread two beads onto the needle.

2. Slide the beads down the thread to the fabric. Take the needle back through the first bead and through the fabric.

3. Pull the thread through and end off on the back of the fabric.

4. Alternatively, use a sequin instead of the first bead.

- Beadpoint - Waste knot -

 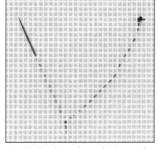

1. Knot the end of the thread. Take it from front to back through the canvas approximately 5cm (2") from your starting point.

2. Pull the thread through. Re-emerge at the starting point.

 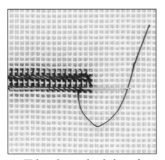

3. Once a section of beading is complete, pull the waste knot away from the canvas and cut it off.

4. Take the tail of thread to the back of the canvas. Thread it into a needle and weave it through the stitching on the back.

Alternating rows of long back stitch and short back stitch minimise the amount of canvas distortion. Long back stitch is equivalent to needlepoint's continental stitch and short back stitch to half cross stitch.

If your beadpoint does require blocking, place a clean cloth over your ironing board or blocking board. Place the beadpoint face down on the cloth. Holding a hot iron just above the beads, apply steam to the entire area. Re-shape the fabric and pin in place. Leave until cool and dry.

Use masking tape to 'bind' the edges of the canvas to prevent the thread from snagging and the fabric from fraying.

Determining the amount of canvas to use

Measure 10cm (4") across the canvas. Count the number of threads within this distance. Divide the number of threads by 4 to determine the canvas count. Repeat the procedure in the opposite direction.

Divide the first canvas count into the number of squares across your chart. This is the finished width of your design. Divide the second canvas count into the number of squares that run up and down your chart. This is the finished depth of your design.

Cut your canvas 5cm (2") wider and higher than the dimensions of the finished design.

- Long back stitch -

Work rows of long back stitch from right to left.

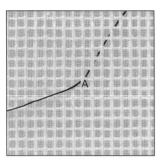

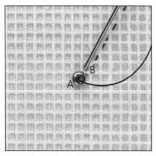

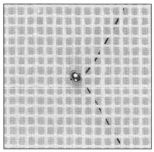

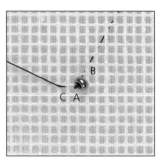

1. Secure the thread and bring it to the front in the lower left hand corner of the first stitch (A).

2. Thread a bead onto the needle. Crossing one canvas intersection, take the needle to the back at B, above and to the right.

3. Pull the thread through.

4. Re-emerge at C, one canvas thread to the left of A.

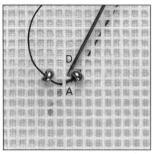

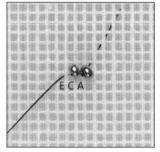

5. Thread a bead onto the needle. Take the needle to the back at D, directly above A.

6. Pull the thread through.

7. Re-emerge at E, one canvas thread to the left of C.

8. Continue across the row in the same manner.

- Short back stitch -

Work rows of short back stitch from left to right.

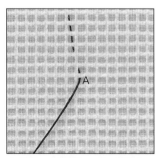

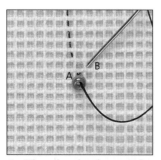

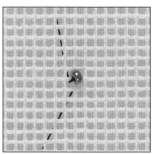

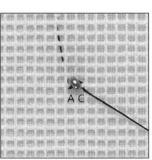

1. Secure the thread and bring it to the front in the lower left hand corner of the first stitch (A).

2. Thread a bead onto the needle. Crossing one canvas intersection, take the needle to the back at B, above and to the right.

3. Pull the thread through.

4. Re-emerge at C, one canvas thread to the right of A.

- *Short back stitch* - continued

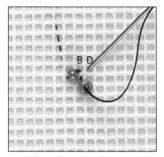

5. Thread a bead onto the needle. Take the needle to the back at D, one canvas thread to the right of B.

6. Pull the thread through.

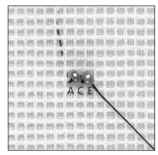

7. Re-emerge at E, one canvas thread to the right of C.

8. Continue across the row in the same manner.

- *Alternating long and short back stitch* -

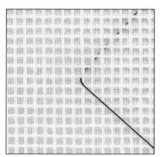

1. First row. Secure the thread and bring it to the front on the right hand side, in the lower left hand corner of the first stitch.

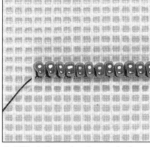

2. Work long back stitch from right to left across the row.

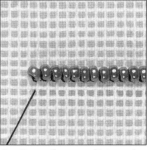

3. Second row. Bring the thread to the front one canvas thread below the lower left hand corner of the previous stitch.

4. Thread a bead onto the needle. Take the needle to the back through the same hole as the lower left hand corner of the second to last stitch in the previous row.

5. Pull the thread through.

6. Continue working short back stitches from left to right across the row.

7. Continue working rows back and forth across the canvas, alternating between long and short back stitch.

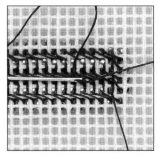

8. End off by weaving the thread through the stitches on the back of the canvas.

- *Attaching a single sequin* -

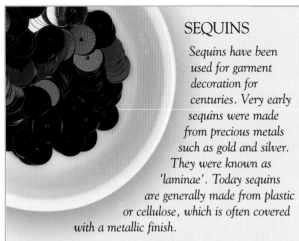

SEQUINS

Sequins have been used for garment decoration for centuries. Very early sequins were made from precious metals such as gold and silver. They were known as 'laminae'. Today sequins are generally made from plastic or cellulose, which is often covered with a metallic finish.

The technical term for a sequin is 'paillette'. This term originated in France and meant any circular disc with a hole in the middle.

During the reign of the Tudor kings in England, sequins were called 'spangles' or 'owe'.

Cupped sequins are also known as 'couvettes'.

During the 17th and 18th centuries sequins were a very popular form of decoration and were combined with metal thread embroidery for the fashionable in the courts of Europe. They were produced in a wide variety of shapes and a particular favourite were 'papillons' or butterflies that were stamped from thin sheets of silver and coloured.

If using a metallic thread to attach sequins, ensure you use a metallic thread especially made for embroidery. Wound metal threads can be quickly stripped of their metal by the sequins.

'ELIZABETHAN DRAGONFLIES' BY JANE NICHOLAS, INSPIRATIONS 32

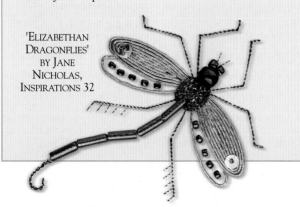

1. Secure the thread on the back of the fabric and bring it to the front at the position for the edge of the sequin.

2. Take the needle to the back through the hole in the sequin.

3. Pull the thread through. Re-emerge on the opposite side of the sequin.

4. Pull the thread through and again take it to the back through the centre hole. End off on the back of the fabric.

5. Variation 1 - three straight stitches.

6. Variation 2 - four straight stitches.

- *Attaching multiple sequins* - Method 1 *(whip stitch)* -

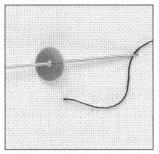

1. Secure the thread on the back of the fabric and bring it to the front. Thread a sequin onto the needle, taking the needle from front to back through the hole.

2. Slide the sequin down the thread to the fabric. Take a tiny horizontal stitch, from right to left, through the fabric at the base of the sequin.

3. Pull the thread through. Flip the sequin so the right side is uppermost.

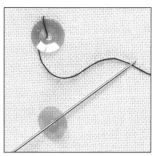

4. Thread a second sequin onto the needle, taking the needle from front to back through the hole.

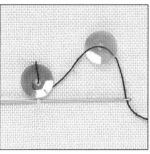

5. Make a tiny horizontal stitch, from right to left, at the base of the first sequin.

6. Pull the thread through. The second sequin will tuck under the first sequin.

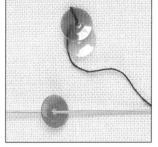

7. Thread a third sequin onto the needle in the same manner as before.

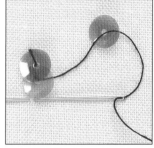

8. Make a tiny horizontal stitch, from right to left, at the base of the second sequin.

9. Pull the thread through. The third sequin will tuck under the second sequin.

10. Continue attaching sequins in the same manner.

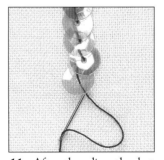

11. After threading the last sequin, take the needle through the fabric as before but do not re-emerge.

12. Pull the thread through and end off on the back of the fabric.

- *Method 2 (back stitch)* -

1. Secure the thread on the back of the fabric. Bring it to the front through the hole in the sequin.

2. Take the needle to the back alongside the right hand edge of the sequin.

3. Pull the thread through. Re-emerge alongside the left hand edge.

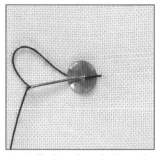

4. Pull the thread through. Take the needle to the back through the centre hole.

5. Pull the thread through. Position a second sequin to the left of the first sequin. Bring the thread to the front through the hole.

6. Take the needle to the back alongside the right hand edge.

7. Pull the thread through. Re-emerge alongside the left hand edge.

8. Pull the thread through. Take the needle to the back through the centre hole.

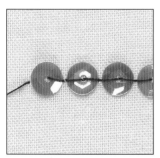

9. Pull the thread through. Continue attaching sequins in the same manner.

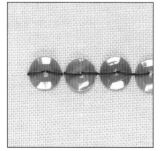

10. After attaching the last sequin, end off the thread on the back of the fabric.

'NAMESAKE' BY JANE NICHOLAS, INSPIRATIONS 36

- *Tambour Work* - *Making a spool holder* -

Place the spool holder on your right if you are right handed and on your left if you are left handed.

TAMBOUR WORK

TAMBOUR IS FRENCH FOR DRUM

This form of embroidery was practised in China thousands of years ago. Eventually it travelled to India, Persia, Turkey and Europe. Tambouring is commonly used for attaching beads and sequins in the fashion houses of European Couture.

Firmly mount the fabric in a hoop or frame that has a stand.

Both hands are needed for the stitching - one to hold the tambour hook above the fabric and the other to hold the thread below the fabric.

ANTIQUE TAMBOUR HOOK

If you have never embroidered with a tambour hook, practice working chain stitches before attaching beads or sequins. Begin stitching on a piece of tulle as it is easy to see the thread path.

Always hold the tambour hook vertically. If it is held at an angle the needle is more likely to catch on the threads of the fabric.

Align the holding screw with the hook of the needle so you always know which way the hook is facing when it is below the fabric.

1. Mark the centre of a piece of wood 12cm (4³/4") square by 1cm (³/8") thick.

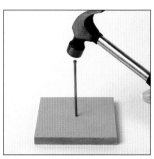

2. Hammer a large nail right through the wood at the marked position.

3. Turn the wood upside down. Place the spool of beading thread onto the nail.

4. Thread a beading needle and pick up the desired beads. Do not thread more than about 70cm (27¹/2") of beads at a time.

5. If picking up sequins, take the needle through the right side first so they will be facing correctly when attached to the fabric.

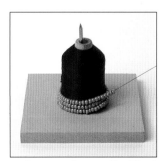

6. Remove the needle. Wind the beads/sequins around the spool.

33

- Preparing the hoop -

Tambour work must be worked in a hoop or frame with a stand or clamp as both hands need to be free - one to hold the hook and the other to hold the thread.

1. Bind the inner ring of the hoop to ensure the fabric can be held very firmly.

2. Trace the design onto the wrong side of the fabric.

3. Position the fabric over the inner ring so the traced design is uppermost.

4. Place the outer ring over the inner ring and tighten to ensure the fabric is smooth and 'drum' tight.

- Securing the thread at the beginning -

1. Keeping the tambour hook vertical and the screw facing away from you, take the hook from top to bottom through the fabric.

2. Hold the thread with your thumb and forefinger beneath the fabric. Lay it over the hook.

3. Raise the hook, pulling a small loop of thread through the fabric.

4. Continue pulling the tail of thread all the way through.

5. Tie a small knot in the tail.

6. Pull the thread from below so the knot lies against the fabric.

- *Ending off the thread* -

1. After covering the required distance, work a chain stitch without adding a bead.

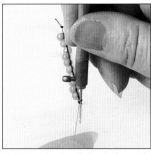

2. Take the hook back through the same hole in the fabric, just outside the previous chain stitch.

3. Pick up the end of the thread and pull a loop through to the top.

4. Keeping the hook through the loop, cut the thread, leaving a 10cm (4") tail.

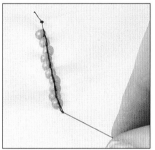

5. Pull the tail to the top and pull firmly until a knot is formed.

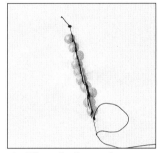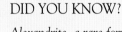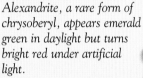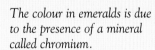

6. Thread the tail into a needle and weave it through the chain stitches.

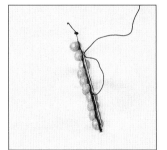

7. Work two tiny back stitches, one on top of the other.

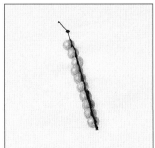

8. Pull the thread through. Trim off excess thread.

DID YOU KNOW?

Alexandrite, a rare form of chrysoberyl, appears emerald green in daylight but turns bright red under artificial light.

Sapphires are very hard and durable. They can scratch any other stone except diamond.

The colour in emeralds is due to the presence of a mineral called chromium.

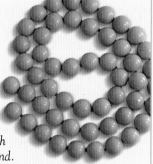

NATURAL
TURQUOISE BEADS

The speckles or veins of gold in lapis-lazuli are not gold but pyrite. Pyrite is also known as fool's gold.

Amethysts are a variety of quartz. Their colour can range from a very deep purple to a pretty pale lilac.

Jet is fossilized coal. It was made popular by Queen Victoria who used it for the beadwork on her mourning clothes after the death of Prince Albert.

Natural turquoise is quite porous and today it is often impregnated with resin to protect and stabilize it.

EMERALDS

- *Attaching beads* -

1. Anchor the thread following the instructions on page 34.

2. Keeping the tambour hook vertical and the screw facing away from you, take the hook from top to bottom through the fabric a short distance from the knot.

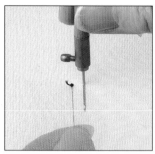

3. Hold the thread with your thumb and forefinger beneath the fabric.

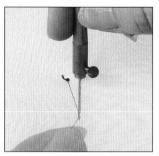

4. Twist the hook anti-clockwise to pick up the thread beneath.

5. Raise the hook, pushing it slightly backwards to enlarge the hole and prevent it from snagging the fabric. The hook should face the knot.

6. Pull a small loop of thread to the surface.

7. Take the hook down through the fabric a short distance away in the same manner as before.

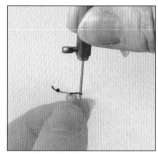

8. Slide a bead (or several beads) up to the fabric and hold in place.

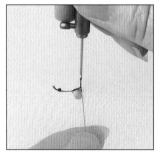

9. Pick up the thread and pull through to the top of the fabric in the same manner as before.

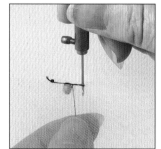

10. Again, take the hook through the fabric a short distance away.

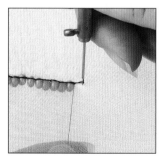

11. Continue attaching beads in the same manner for the required distance.

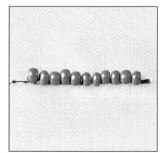

12. End off following the instructions on page 35.

- *Attaching sequins* -

1. Anchor the thread following the instructions on page 34.

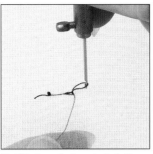

2. Work a chain stitch following steps 2 - 7 on page 36.

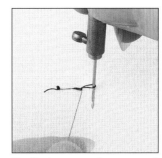

3. Begin to work a second chain stitch the same length as the radius of your threaded sequins.

4. As you raise the hook, tighten the bottom thread so the loop of the chain stitch slides back to the base of the stitch.

5. Take the hook through the previous stitch.

6. Work a small chain stitch. This will lock the previous stitch.

7. Slide a sequin up to the fabric and hold in place.

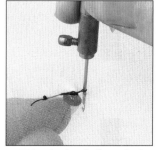

8. Take the hook through the fabric to make a stitch the same length as the radius of the sequin.

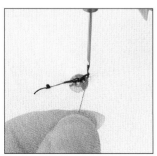

9. Pick up the thread in the same manner as before and pull through to the top of the fabric to anchor the sequin.

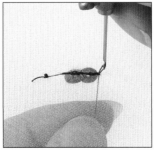

10. Again, take the hook through the fabric. Repeat steps 3 - 9 to attach a second sequin.

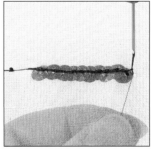

11. Continue attaching sequins in the same manner for the required distance.

12. End off following the instructions on page 35.

Design
Gallery

The Royal Society of Entomology
cordially invites you to attend
the Society's Annual Luncheon

Odonata Restaurant and Garden
September First, 1 PM

- STARFLOWER -

By Karen Torrisi of New South Wales

ORDER OF WORK

Trace the design onto the right side of the background fabric using your chosen method. Mount the fabric in the hoop.

Flower

Outline the petals with two rows of champagne bugle beads. Work a single row around the star-shaped centre in the same manner.

Attach the rhinestone to the centre, stitching in a cross formation through the channels on the back. Surround this with a circle of eight beads. Cover the remaining section of the centre with scattered champagne bugle beads.

Fill the petals with scattered cream bugle beads, attaching one bead at a time.

FINISHING

Place the finished embroidery face down on a well padded surface and press gently around the design. Take care not to press over the beaded area.

THIS DESIGN USES

Beading

REQUIREMENTS

Beads

Bugle beads 2mm (1/16″) long

A = champagne

B = cream

Claw set rhinestone 4mm (3/16″) wide

C = crystal AB

Supplies

Beading thread

Beading needle

Background fabric

Embroidery hoop 15cm (6″) wide

COLOUR KEY

All stitching is worked using two strands of beading thread.

Flower

Outlines = A

Petals = B

Centre = A and C

- PANDORA'S GARDEN -

By Liz Vickery of South Australia

Beading, Pistil stitch, Ribbon stitch

REQUIREMENTS

Beads

Delica 11/0 glass beads

A = DBR624 pearl light pink

B = DBR689 semi-matte silverlined light grey-green

C = DBR829 satin light alabaster/green

Maria George 15/0 Ceylon beads

D = 4112 gold

Maria George 11/0 antique beads

E = 9102 cyclamen

Czech fire polished beads 4mm (3/16") wide

F = amethyst AB x 24

G = light amethyst AB x 23

H = French rose AB x 29

I = mauve x 23

J = crystal AB x 27

Swarovski rondelles 3mm (1/8") wide

K = light amethyst x 8

L = crystal AB x 32

Bead cap 4mm (3/16") wide

M = silver x 18

Claw set diamantes 4mm (3/16") wide

N = crystal x 5

Diamante 3mm (1/8") wide

O = crystal x 1

Embroidery thread & ribbon

Kreinik very fine metallic braid

P = 001 silver

Hand-dyed silk ribbon 7mm (5/16") wide

Q = green

Supplies

Hand-dyed lace motifs

Silver butterfly finding

Beading thread

Beading needle

No. 9 crewel needle

No. 24 chenille needle

Background fabric

Embroidery hoop 20cm (8") wide

Clear craft glue

Two-pack glue (eg Araldite)

Disposable cloth

ORDER OF WORK

Mount the fabric in the hoop. Using small droplets of clear craft glue, fix the lace motifs to the right side of the fabric. Allow the glue to dry.

Use the beading needle for attaching the beads, the chenille needle for the ribbon embroidery and the crewel needle for the thread embroidery.

Large flowers

Attach a diamante to the centre of each large flower, taking the stitches through the two channels on the back. Bring the thread to the front near the centre to begin beading a petal. Thread a rondelle and then a fire polished bead onto the needle.

Secure the beads by taking the thread through them twice. Repeat for all remaining petals.

Medium flowers

Work the centres following the step-by-step instructions on page 42. Attach a single fire polished bead over each lace petal.

Beaded leaves

Attach a single string of light grey-green beads along the middle of the small leaves. Vary the number of beads to fit the length of each leaf.

Bead the large leaves following the step-by-step instructions on page 61. Use the light grey-green beads for the first row and the light alabaster/green beads for the second row. Again, vary the number of beads to fit the length of each leaf.

Forget-me-nots

Secure a single gold bead at the centre of each flower. Surround these with a circle of six beads. Add two light grey-green beads for leaves.

Ribbon leaves

Embroider the ribbon stitch leaves among the large and medium flowers in pairs or groups of three.

Butterfly

Stitch two pistil stitches for the antennae. Attach a bead cap for the head. Secure by taking the thread through the filigree of the bead cap and re-emerging on the opposite side. Work a second stitch at right angles to the first stitch. Attach the butterfly finding so the antennae are aligned with the head.

FINISHING

Place the finished embroidery face down on a well padded surface and press gently around the design. Take care not to press over the beaded areas.

Cut a small hole in the disposable cloth. Place the cloth over the design so the hole is positioned over a flower centre. Mix the two-pack glue following the manufacturer's instructions. Glue a diamante into the exposed bead cap. Repeat for all remaining flower centres. Allow to dry.

COLOUR KEY

All thread embroidery is worked with one strand of thread. Use a doubled strand of beading thread when attaching the diamantes, rondelles and fire polished beads, and a single strand for all other beading.

Large flowers

Centres = N

Petals of flower 1 = H and L

Petals of flower 2 = F and L

Petals of flower 3 = J and K

Petals of flower 4 = G and L

Petals of flower 5 = I and L

Medium flowers

Centres = E and M

Petals = F, G, H, I or J

Forget-me-nots

Centres = D

Petals = A

Leaves

Large leaves = B and C

Small leaves = B

Forget-me-not leaves = B

Ribbon leaves = Q (ribbon stitch)

Butterfly

Antennae = P (pistil stitch)

Head = M and O

- Flower centre with bead cap -

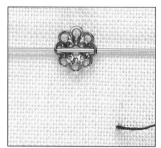

1. Bring the thread to the front at the flower centre. Take the needle through the filigree of a bead cap, re-emerging on the opposite side.

2. Pull the thread through. Take the needle to the back of the fabric close to where it emerged from the bead cap.

3. Pull the thread through. Re-emerge on one side of the bead cap, halfway between the ends of the previous stitch.

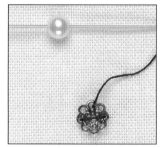

4. Take the needle through the filigree and then thread a bead onto the needle.

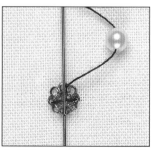

5. Take the needle through the filigree on the opposite side.

6. Pull the thread through. Take it to the back of the fabric and end off.

- JAPONICA -

By Anna Scott of South Australia

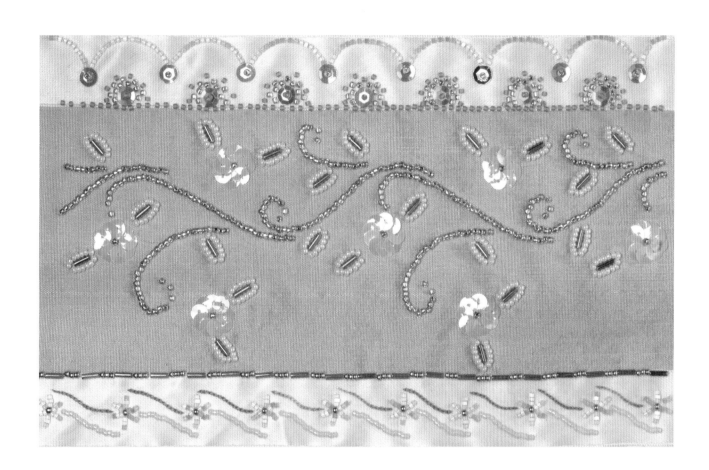

THIS DESIGN USES

Beading, Chain stitch

REQUIREMENTS

Beads & sequins

Delica 11/0 glass beads

A = DBR676 satin lustre white

B = DBR863 transparent matte shark grey AB

11/0 glass seed beads

C = pearl

D = champagne AB

Mill Hill glass seed beads

E = 00123 cream

Mill Hill antique beads

F = 03005 platinum rose

Mill Hill small bugle beads 6mm (1/4")

G = 72053 nutmeg

Flat sequins 6mm (1/4") wide

H = ivory

Cup sequins 6mm (1/4") wide

I = champagne AB

Embroidery thread

Watercolours by Caron

J = 113 teak

Supplies

Beading thread

Beading needle

No. 9 crewel needle

Background fabric

ORDER OF WORK

Trace the design onto the right side of the background fabric using your chosen method.

Use the crewel needle when stitching with the embroidery thread and the beading needle for attaching the beads and sequins.

Central design

Begin by couching beads along each stem. Secure beads individually at the curled ends, spacing them slightly apart. Work the sequin flowers following the step-by-step instructions on page 45.

Attach a single bugle bead for the middle of each leaf. Along each side, attach a string of 6 - 7 cream beads.

Upper band

Using the back stitch method, attach scallops of satin lustre white beads along the upper edge. Add a sequin at the peak of each scallop, holding it in place with a platinum rose bead.

Stitch a line of shark grey beads along the lower edge, attaching each bead separately and spacing them apart. Add sequins at the positions indicated on the pattern, holding them in place with shark grey beads. Surround each sequin with a scattering of champagne and shark grey beads.

Lower band

Embroider the upper waved lines with chain stitch and couch pearl beads along the lower lines.

Stitch a six-petalled flower between each pair of waved lines. Leaving a tiny space at the centre, work each petal with three satin lustre white beads. Add a platinum rose bead to the centre of each flower.

Along the upper edge, work a line of bugle and seed beads. Alternate one bugle bead with three seed beads along the row.

COLOUR KEY

All stitching is worked using one strand of thread.

Central design

Stems = D

Flower petals = H

Flower centres = D

Leaves = E and G

Upper band

Scallops = A

Scallop peaks = F and I

Lower line = B

Sequin and bead cluster = B, D and I

Lower band

Upper waved lines = J (chain stitch)

Lower waved lines = C

Flower petals = A

Flower centres = F

Upper line = F and G

- *Sequin Flower* -

You may find it easier to turn the fabric as you progressively attach each sequin.

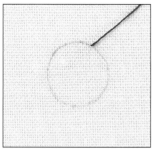

1. Mark a circle on the right side of the fabric as a guideline. Secure the thread on the back of the fabric and bring it to the front on the marked line.

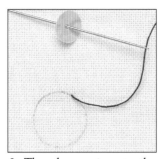

2. Thread a sequin onto the needle, taking the needle from front to back through the hole.

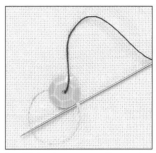

3. Slide the sequin down the thread to the fabric. Take a tiny stitch, from right to left, across the marked line at the edge of the sequin.

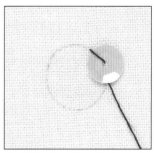

4. Pull the thread through. Flip the sequin so the right side is uppermost.

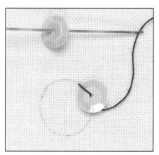

5. Thread a second sequin onto the needle, taking the needle from front to back through the hole.

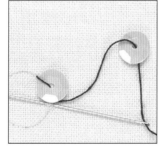

6. Make a tiny stitch, from right to left, across the marked line at the edge of the first sequin.

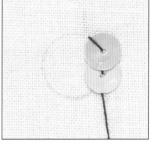

7. Pull the thread through. The second sequin will tuck under the first sequin.

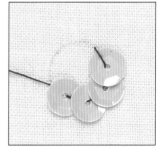

8. Continue attaching sequins along the marked line in the same manner.

9. The last sequin will overlap the first sequin.

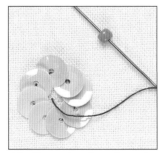

10. Bring the thread to the front in the middle of the sequins. Slip a bead onto the needle.

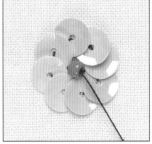

11. Attach the bead with a back stitch.

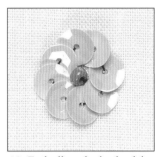

12. End off on the back of the fabric.

- VICTORIANA -
By Liz Vickery of South Australia

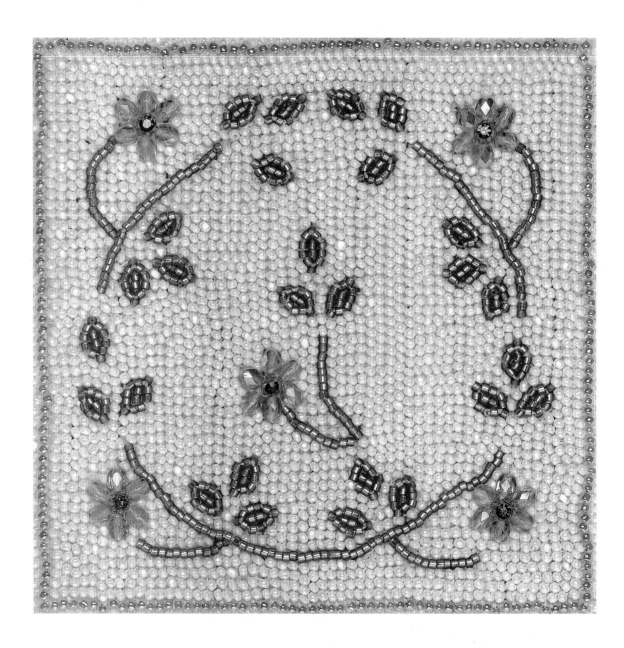

Beading, Beadpoint

REQUIREMENTS

Beads

Delica 11/0 glass beads

A = DBR689 semi-matte silverlined light grey-green

Maria George 11/0 glass beads

B = 6102 ivory

C = 6109 lilac

Czech fire polished beads 4mm (³/₁₆″) wide

D = French rose AB x 30

Diamantes 2.5mm (¹/₈″) wide

E = amethyst x 5

Bead caps 4mm (³/₁₆″) wide

F = gold x 5

Supplies

Beading thread

No. 10 straw (milliner's) needle

14 count penelope canvas

Disposable coth

Water-soluble fabric marker

Two-pack glue (eg Araldite)

Embroidery hoop 20cm (8″) wide

ORDER OF WORK

Trace the design onto the right side of the background fabric using your chosen method. Mount the fabric in the hoop.

Stems and leaves

Bead the stems first, adding up to six beads at a time. Once a stem is complete, take the thread back through all the beads and pull firmly to help align them.

Stitch the leaves following the step-by-step instructions on page 61. Use six beads for the first side and four for the second. Secure two beads inside each leaf outline.

Flowers

Attach a bead cap for the centre of each flower. Secure by taking the thread through the filigree of the bead cap and re-emerging on the opposite side. Work a second stitch at right angles to the first stitch.

Bring the thread to the front near a centre to begin beading the petals. Securing the beads by taking the thread through them twice, add a bead next to the centre and then one on the opposite side. Repeat this two more times so there are six petals. Repeat for all remaining flowers.

Background and border

Mark the centre of the design with a pin. Count out thirty squares in each direction from the centre pin. Mark the fabric at each point with the water-soluble fabric marker.

Rule lines through the marks to form a square *(diag 1)*.

Beginning in the upper left corner, work the background and border in beadpoint following the step-by-step instructions on pages 27 - 29.

	— 30 beads —	— 30 beads —
		30 beads
		30 beads

Diag 1

FINISHING

If necessary, block the beading following the instructions on page 27. Cut a small hole in the disposable cloth. Place the cloth over the design so the hole is positioned over a flower centre. Mix the two-pack glue following the manufacturer's instructions. Glue a diamante into the exposed bead cap. Repeat for all remaining flower centres. Allow to dry.

COLOUR KEY

All stitching is worked using a double strand of beading thread.

Leaves = A

Stems = A

Flowers

Centres = E and F

Petals = D

Background = B

Border = B and C

- SIAM -

By Liz Vickery of South Australia

WHENCE IS YONDER FLOWER SO STRANGELY BRIGHT?

WOULD THE SUNSET'S LAST REFLECTED SHINE

FLAME SO RED FROM THAT DEAD FLUSH OF LIGHT?

Dora Read Goodale

THIS DESIGN USES

Beading, Ribbon stitch

REQUIREMENTS

Beads

11/0 glass seed beads

A = silverlined garnet

Bugle beads 2mm (1/16″) long

B = green iris

*Czech fire polished beads
8mm (7/16″) wide*

C = Siam x 12

Czech glass rondelles 4mm (3/16″) wide

D = Siam x 30

Diamantes 3mm (1/8″) wide

E = topaz x 5

Bead caps 4mm (3/16″) wide

F = gold x 5

Embroidery ribbon

Organza ribbon 10mm (3/8″) wide

G = green

Supplies

Beading thread

Beading needle

No. 24 chenille needle

Background fabric

Embroidery hoop 20cm (8″) wide

Two-pack glue (eg Araldite)

Disposable cloth

ORDER OF WORK

Trace the design onto the right side of the background fabric using your chosen method. Mount the fabric in the hoop.

Use the beading needle for attaching the beads and the chenille needle for the ribbon embroidery.

Stems

Using the back stitch method, work all the stems first.

Small flowers

Attach a bead cap for the centre of one flower. Secure by taking the thread through the filigree of the bead cap and re-emerging on the opposite side. Work a second stitch at right angles to the first stitch. Repeat for the two remaining small flowers.

To begin the petal outlines, work six evenly spaced spokes radiating from the centre. Use three seed beads to form each spoke. Finish the petals following the instructions on pages 54 - 55 and using six seed beads for each petal tip. Couch the tip of each petal between the third and fourth beads.

Attach a rondelle inside each petal outline.

Large flowers

Stitch the centre and the spokes in the same manner as the small flowers. Finish the tips of the inner petals in the same manner as before but use seven beads for each one.

Attach a rondelle inside each petal outline.

Bring the thread to the front alongside the fourth bead of one petal tip. Take the thread through this bead and add nine seed beads. Take the needle through the fourth bead of the next petal's tip and add a further nine beads. Continue in this manner until all the outer petal outlines are worked. Couch the tip of each petal between the fifth and sixth beads. Using doubled thread, attach a large fire polished bead inside each outer petal outline.

Repeat for the remaining flower.

Ribbon leaves

Embroider the ribbon stitch leaves in pairs or groups of three.

FINISHING

Place the finished embroidery face down on a well padded surface and press gently around the design. Take care not to press over the beaded and ribbon embroidered areas.

Cut a small hole in the disposable cloth. Place the cloth over the design so the hole is positioned over a flower centre. Mix the two-pack glue following the manufacturer's instructions. Glue a diamante into the exposed bead cap. Repeat for all remaining flower centres. Allow to dry.

COLOUR KEY

Use a doubled strand of beading thread when attaching the rondelles and fire polished beads, and a single strand for all other beading.

Large flowers

Centre = E and F

Petal outlines = A

Inner petals = D

Outer petals = C

Small flowers

Centre = E and F

Petal outlines = A

Petals = D

Stems = B

Leaves = G (ribbon stitch)

- MARIE ANTOINETTE -

By Helan Pearce of Victoria

THIS DESIGN USES

Tambour beading

REQUIREMENTS

Beads

Size 1 sequins 3mm (1/8") wide

A = white

Size 2 sequins 4mm (3/16") wide

B = clear AB

Delica 11/0 glass beads

C = DBR672 off-white satin

Pearls 2mm (1/16") wide

D = white

Supplies

Beading thread

Very fine cornaly needle
(tambour hook)

Beading needle

Background fabric

Fine water-soluble fabric marker

Tambour hoop 15cm (6") wide

ORDER OF WORK

Use the beading needle for stringing
the beads and sequins and the
tambour hook for attaching them to
the fabric.

Trace the design onto the wrong
side of the fabric using your chosen
method.

Place the fabric firmly in the hoop
with the wrong side facing you.

Working the pearls

See pages 33 - 37 for the step-by-
step instructions on tambour work.

Use the close-up photograph and
the embroidery design as a guide to
bead placement.

Leaving a tail of thread on top of
the work and starting at the upper
scroll, attach the pearls. Work the
outer scroll next, beginning at one
side of the upper scroll. Repeat for
the other side. Attach the lattice
work of pearls inside the design.

Attach the sequins around the outer
scroll, keeping them close to the
pearls.

Oval shapes

Outline the small oval shapes using
the off-white satin beads and
starting each one at the top.

Fill in the shapes with the tiny
sequins, working from the centre
out in a spiral manner.

Centre rose

Outline and fill the rose in a similar
manner to the ovals.

COLOUR KEY

All stitching is worked using
one strand of beading thread.

Top scroll = D

Outer Scroll = B and D

Lattice = D

Ovals outline = A

Ovals filling = C

Rose outline = A

Rose filling = C

Hint

*If tiny beads are sticking to the sides
of a bag or lid due to static electricity,
gently blow on them. The warm, moist
air will cause them to drop away.*

'SILKEN TOUCH' BY ANNIE HUMPHRIS,
INSPIRATIONS 34

- MAGNOLIA -

By Liz Vickery of South Australia

THIS DESIGN USES

Beading

REQUIREMENTS

Beads

Delica 11/0 glass beads

A = DBR373 matte metallic under leaf green

B = DBR672 satin off-white

C = DBR852 transparent matte light topaz AB

D = DBR853 transparent matte dark topaz AB

Maria George 15/0 Ceylon beads

E = 4101 ivory

Maria George 11/0 glass beads

F = 6102 ivory

Maria George 11/0 lustre beads

G = 7016 amber

Czech 14/0 Unica beads

H = matte green iris

Supplies

Beading thread

Beading needle

Background fabric

Embroidery hoop 25cm (10") wide

ORDER OF WORK

Trace the design onto the right side of the background fabric using your chosen method. Mount the fabric in the hoop.

Stems and leaves

Using the back stitch method and the larger green beads, outline the leaves. Change to the dark topaz beads, and work the stems in the same manner. Add the leaf veins using the smaller green beads.

Flowers

Stitch the large flower following the step-by-step instructions on pages 54 - 55.

Work the centre of the small upper left flower in the same manner as the centre of the large flower. For all remaining flower centres, attach a centre bead and surround this with a circle of eight amber beads. Work the petal outlines in a similar fashion to those of the large flower.

FINISHING

Place the finished embroidery face down on a well padded surface and press gently around the design. Take care not to press over the beaded areas.

COLOUR KEY

All stitching is worked using one strand of beading thread.

Leaves

Outlines = A

Veins = H

Stems = D

Large flower

Centre = B and G

Petal outlines = F

Petal filling = C

Small flowers

Centre of upper left flower = B, C and G

Centres of remaining flowers = C and G

Petal outlines = E

Magnolia macrophylla

A decidious tree growing to 10m by 10m at a slow rate.

The flowers are hermaphrodites (have both male and female organs) and are pollinated by beetles.

Edible Uses
None known.

Medicinal Uses
Odontalgic; Stomachic.

An infusion of the bark has been used in the treatment of stomach aches or cramps. A hot infusion of the bark has been snuffed for treating sinus problems and has been held in the mouth for treating toothache.

Other Uses
Wood - soft, light, not strong, close-grained. Used for flooring, cabinet making etc.

Flowers
The flowers are large 25 - 36cm (10 - 14") and showy, with several long creamy white petals, very fragrant.

Fruit
Egg shaped rose coloured fruit.

- *Large cream flower* -

1. Centre. Attach a single bead for the middle of the flower centre.

2. Surround the bead with a circle of eight beads.

3. Work a circle of twelve beads around the previous circle.

4. Petals. Bring the thread to the front near the centre and slip seven beads onto the needle.

5. Push beads close together and take the thread to the back after the last bead. Work a couching stitch between the third and fourth beads.

6. Work eight more spokes in the same manner.

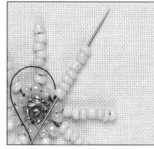

7. Using a new thread, bring it to the front at the base of one spoke. Take the needle through the spoke.

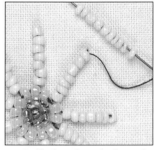

8. Pull the thread through. Slip ten beads onto the needle.

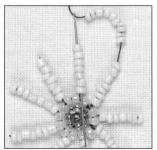

9. Slide the beads down the thread. Starting at the tip, take the needle through the adjacent spoke.

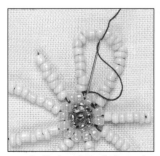

10. Pull the thread through. Take the needle to the back of the fabric.

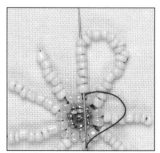

11. Pull the thread through. Re-emerge a very short distance away and take the needle back through the same seven beads.

12. Working in an anti-clockwise direction, work the tips of the remaining petals in the same manner.

- *Large cream flower* - continued

13. Work a couching stitch between the fifth and sixth beads of each petal tip.

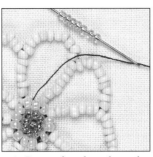

14. Bring the thread to the front inside one petal near the base. Slip seven beads onto the needle.

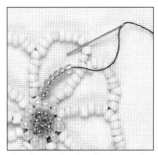

15. Slide the beads down the thread. Take the needle to the back near the tip of the petal.

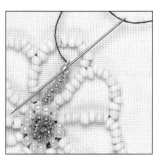

16. Pull the thread through. Re-emerge a very short distance away. Take the needle through the last bead added.

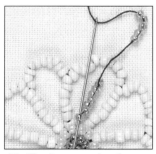

17. Slip five more beads onto the needle. Take the needle through the very first bead added.

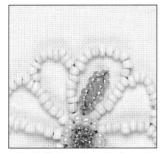

18. Pull the thread through and take it to the back of the fabric.

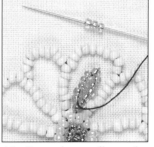

19. Bring the needle to the front, inside the previous beads, near the base. Pull the thread through. Slip three beads onto the needle.

20. Take the needle to the back of the fabric inside the previous beads near the tip.

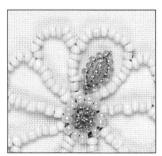

21. Pull the thread through.

22. Fill the remaining petals in the same manner.

'THE DRAGONFLY' BY JANE NICHOLAS, INSPIRATIONS 41

- DRAGONFLY -

By Helan Pearce of Victoria

REQUIREMENTS

Beads

Delica 11/0 glass beads

A = DBC23 metallic light bronze iris

B = DBR31 metallic bright gold

Bugle beads 2.5mm (1/8") long

C = gold

Round crystal 6mm (1/4") wide

D = dark amethyst AB x 1

Crystal flowers 6mm (1/4") wide

E = purple x 2

Supplies

Fine tulle

Water-soluble fabric

Beading thread

Beading needle

Black fine permanent marker

Embroidery hoop 20cm (8") wide

ORDER OF WORK

Trace the design onto the water-soluble fabric using your chosen method.

Place the water-soluble fabric over the tulle and tack around the outer edge and close to the outline of the dragonfly. Avoid tacking over the design itself as it is hard to remove tacking once the beading is complete.

With the design uppermost, place the fabric in the hoop.

When working on tulle, it is important to start and end off your thread carefully by weaving the thread through the stitches on the back of your work.

Dragonfly

Wings

Following the outline of the design, attach a row of beads around each wing.

Following the instructions on page 58 and using the photograph and the stitch direction diagrams as a guide, fill in the top and inner areas of the upper wings and the inner portions of the lower wings. This will give a raised effect.

Fill in the centre of the upper wings with the gold bugle beads. Attach the purple crystal flower in the lower corners of the upper wings with a single bronze iris bead.

Fill in the remaining portion of the lower wings with gold beads using the same three beads picot method.

Body

Following the step-by-step instructions on page 19 and using two beads, outline the top of the body using the bronze iris beads. Outline the lower body with the gold beads attaching one bead at a time.

Reversing the colours, fill in the body attaching one bead at a time. Use gold for the top and bronze iris for the lower end.

Thorax and head

Attach the round crystal in the centre. Couch a circle of beads around the crystal. Attach individual beads around the circle of beads. Add two picots of three beads each for the eyes.

Heart shape

Using multiples of two, attach the beads around the outer edge of the heart shape, forming little scallops.

FINISHING

Carefully cut away as much of the water-soluble fabric as possible. Place the beaded piece into a bowl of tepid water to dissolve the remaining water-soluble fabric.

Rinse in a clean bowl of water to make sure all traces have been removed.

Dry flat on a tea towel. If you find that the tulle feels stiff or sticky, repeat the process.

Cut away the tulle close to the beaded heart shape.

COLOUR KEY

All stitching is worked using one strand of beading thread.

Dragonfly

Wings

Wing outlines = A

Upper wings = A, C and E

Lower wings = A and B

Body

Upper body outline = A

Lower body outline = B

Inner body = A and B

Thorax = A and D

Eyes = A

Heart shape = A

Hint

To make sure you are beading through the tulle and not just the water-soluble fabric, check the wrong side as you work.

Ensure the holes in the tulle are smaller than the beads you are using so they cannot be pulled through to the back.

'ELIZABETHAN DRAGONFLIES' BY JANE NICHOLAS, INSPIRATIONS 32

- Bead Picots -

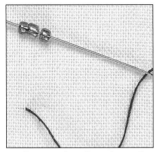

1. Secure the thread on the back of the fabric and bring it to the front. Thread the required number of beads onto the needle.

2. Slide the beads down the thread to the fabric. Take the needle to the back of the fabric a short distance away (less than the length of the strung beads).

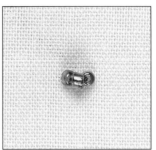

3. Pull the thread through. The beads will remain slightly raised.

4. Re-emerge very close to where the thread went to the back of the fabric.

5. Thread the same number of beads onto the needle again.

6. Work the stitch in the same manner as before.

7. Continue attaching groups of beads in the same manner, allowing them to overlap if desired.

8. After attaching the last group, end off on the back of the fabric.

Did you know?

In the English language, the word bead comes from the Anglo-Saxon word 'bede', meaning prayer. Gradually the name transferred from the prayer itself to the rosaries on which the prayers were counted.

During the nineteenth century, glass beads were imported into England from Germany and Italy. Victorian women ordered their beads by the pound rather than the ounce, resulting in the name 'pound beads'.

- DUCHESS -

By Liz Vickery of South Australia

THIS DESIGN USES

Beading

REQUIREMENTS

Beads

Delica 11/0 glass beads

A = DBR672 satin off-white

Maria George 15/0 Ceylon beads

B = 4101 ivory

Pearls 3mm (1/8") wide

C = cream

*Czech fire polished beads
3mm (1/8") wide*

D = crystal

Swarovski rondelles 4mm (3/16") wide

E = crystal

Bead caps 4mm (3/16") wide

F = gold

Supplies

Cream lace motifs

Beading thread

Beading needle

Background fabric

Embroidery hoop 25cm (10") wide

Clear craft glue

ORDER OF WORK

Mount the fabric in the hoop. Using small droplets of glue, fix the lace motifs to the right side of the fabric. Allow the glue to dry.

Leaves and fronds

Stitching over the lace, stitch the leaves following the step-by-step instructions on page 61. Use five beads for the first row and three for the second row.

Fill the lace fronds with two rows of off-white beads. Add a pearl to the tips of those fronds that curl into a circle.

Flowers

Work the centres of all flowers following the step-by-step instructions on page 42.

On each small flower, attach a crystal rondelle inside the lace petal. Repeat for the inner petals of the large flowers. To complete the outer petals of the large flowers, attach three strings of beads, inside each petal half, each consisting of three Ceylon beads and three Delica beads.

Using the 3mm (1/8") polished beads, work the inner petals of the medium flowers in the same manner as the large flowers. Fill each half of the outer petals with two strings of beads, each consisting of two Ceylon beads and two Delica beads.

Cornucopias

Fill each cornucopia with pairs of satin off-white beads back stitched in place. Attach a pearl bead inside each curled end.

FINISHING

Place the finished embroidery face down on a well padded surface and press gently around the design. Take care not to press over the beaded areas.

COLOUR KEY

All stitching is worked using a doubled strand of beading thread.

Leaves and fronds

Leaves = A

Fronds = A

Frond curls = C

Large flowers

Centres = C and F

Inner petals = E

Outer petals = A and B

Medium flowers

Centres = C and F

Inner petals = D

Outer petals = A and B

Small flowers

Centre = C and F

Petals = E

Cornucopias

Filling = A

Ends = C

NECKLACE WITH AUSTRIAN RHINESTONES

- Leaf -

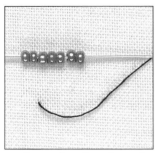

1. Bring the thread to the front at the base of the leaf. Thread the required number of beads onto the needle.

2. Slide the beads down the thread to the fabric. Take the needle to the back at the end of the last bead. This is the tip of the leaf.

3. Pull the thread through. Re-emerge a very short distance away near the end of the last bead.

4. Pull the thread through. Take the needle through the last bead added.

5. Thread onto the needle, two beads less than the first row.

6. Take the needle through the very first bead added.

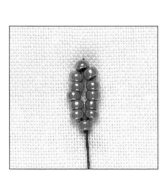

7. Pull the thread through.

8. Take the thread to the back of the fabric and end off.

Swarovski

In 1895, Swarovski was founded by Daniel Swarovski in Wattens, Austria. Daniel and his three sons revolutionised the quality of cut crystal and their crystal bead formula was perfected around the turn of the 20th century. Each bead is fired using a combination of quartz sand and natural minerals, then cooled slowly to avoid causing stress to the crystal. The beads contain 32% lead compared to most other types which contain only 24%. This, as well as their secret manufacturing process, produces crystals with a diamond like brilliance.

In cooperation with Christian Dior, Swarovski created the Aurora Borealis finish in 1955. This spectacular rainbow coating transformed beading.

Today, Swarovski is still a family owned business, but employs over 9,000 people.

- PUNICA -

By Anna Scott of South Australia

THIS DESIGN USES

Beading, Chain stitch
Padded satin stitch, Split stitch

REQUIREMENTS

Beads

Delica 11/0 glass beads

A = DBR114 transparent
silver grey lustre

Mill Hill glass seed beads

B = 00367 garnet

C = 02012 royal plum

Maria George 11/0 antique beads

D = 9142 peacock

Bugle beads 5mm (¹/₄") long

E = silver

Auroa 8/0 beads

F = crystal iris

Embroidery threads

Madeira stranded silk

G = 1707 green-grey

Supplies

Beading thread

Beading needle

No. 8 crewel needle

Background fabric

Embroidery hoop 20cm (8") wide

ORDER OF WORK

Trace the design onto the right side
of the background fabric using your
chosen method. Mount the fabric in
the hoop.

Use the crewel needle when stitching
with the stranded silk and the beading needle for attaching the beads.

Main stems and sepals

Stitch the flower and fruit stems
with chain stitch and outline the
sepals with split stitch. Embroider
satin stitches inside the outline of
one sepal for padding. Cover these
stitches and the outline with a
second layer of satin stitch lying in
the opposite direction. Repeat for
all remaining sepals.

Attach a silver grey lustre bead
within each chain stitch, using the
back stitch method.

Small stems and twigs

Spacing the beads slightly and using
the back stitch method, attach beads
for the remaining stems. Add a
peacock bead to the tip of each one.
Surround these with three bugle
beads. Stitch the twigs in the
middle of the design in the same
manner, omitting the bugle beads.

Flowers

Attach a row of silver grey lustre
beads along the outer edge of one
flower. Alternating bead colours,
work two rows each with the garnet
and royal plum beads. Fill in the
space at the base with garnet beads
and add a crystal iris bead over the
sepals. Repeat for the second flower

At the top of each flower. Secure
two bugle beads and one crystal iris
bead for the stamens.

Pomegranate

Outline the pomegranate in the
same manner as the flowers. Fill the

outer section on each side with three
rows of royal plum beads and then
outline the inner section with garnet
beads. Scatter several crystal iris
seed beads in the inner section. Add
the stamens at the top in the same
manner as those on the flowers.

FINISHING

Place the finished embroidery face
down on a padded surface and press
gently around the design. Take care
not to press over the beaded areas.

COLOUR KEY

All stitching is worked using
one strand of thread.

Stems and twigs

Main stems = G (chain stitch), A

Small stems = A

Tips of small stems = D

Twigs = E

Flowers

Petal outlines = A

Petals = B and C

Sepals = G (split stitch,
padded satin stitch)

Stamens = E and F

Pomegranate

Outline = A

Outer sections = C

Inner section outline = B

Inner section = F

Sepals = G (split stitch,
padded satin stitch)

Stamens = E and F

- ROSELINE -

By Liz Vickery of South Australia

REQUIREMENTS

Beads

Delica 11/0 glass beads

A = DBR624 pearl light pink

Maria George 15/0 Ceylon beads

B = 4112 gold

Czech glass hearts 4mm (3/16″) wide

C = roseline

Pearls 3mm (1/8″) wide

D = light rose

Bead caps 4mm (3/16″) wide

E = gold

Supplies

Beading thread

No. 10 straw (milliner's) needle

Background fabric with pintucks
3cm (1 1/4″) apart

ORDER OF WORK

Beaded pintucks

Whip the pearl light pink beads
along each side of the pintucks. To
do this, secure the thread at the top
left hand corner. Take the thread
under the first stitch of the pintuck.
Thread a bead onto the needle and
then take the thread under the next
stitch of the pintuck. Continue in
this manner to the end of the
pintuck (*diag 1*).

Diag 1

Turn the fabric and repeat along the
other side of the pintuck. Whip
beads to all the remaining pintucks
in the same manner.

Attach a single gold bead at each
intersection.

Flowers

Work the centres following the
step-by-step instructions on page 42.
Working in a clockwise direction
and with the base of the heart
towards the centre, attach five heart
beads around each centre. Secure
the beads by taking the thread
through them twice.

FINISHING

Place the finished embroidery face
down on a well padded surface and
press gently.

COLOUR KEY

Use a doubled strand of beading
thread for the flowers and a
single strand for the pintucks.

Beaded pintucks

Along pintucks = A

At intersections = B

Flowers

Centres = D and E

Petals = C

- RUBY -

By Judith Coombe of South Australia

THIS DESIGN USES

Back stitch, Beading
Detached chain, Stab stitch
Stem stitch, Straight stitch

REQUIREMENTS

Beads

Delica 11/0 glass beads

A = DBR331 matte metallic yellow gold

B = DBR353 matte dark cream

C = DBR371 matte metallic olive green

D = DBR690 semi-matte silverlined dark grey-green

E = DBR883 opaque matte cream AB

F = DBR902 lined crystal/shimmering rose pink

11/0 glass seed beads

G = silverlined crystal

H = pale pink

I = yellow iris AB

Judith and Kathryn flower beads

J = frosted six-petalled flower 25mm (1") wide x 1

K = pale peach five-petalled flowers 15mm (5/8") wide x 4

L = frosted four-petalled flowers 7mm (5/16") wide x 17

M = pink five-petalled flowers 7mm (5/16") wide x 3

N = pink five-petalled flowers 6mm (1/4") wide x 4

O = pink five-petalled flowers 12mm (1/2") wide x 2

P = butterfly 10mm (3/8") wide x 1

Embroidery threads

Raiman rayon machine embroidery threads

Q = RT104 calico

R = RT118 sand

S = RT186 bluegum

T = RT419 olive

U = RT460 dusty pink

Madeira embroidery floss

V = 2101 cream

W = 2102 caramel

Supplies

'Ruby' silk print from Judith and Kathryn Designs

Pellon 30cm (12") square

Lace motif

Beading thread

Beading needle

No. 10 sharp needle

No. 8 sharp needle

Teabag

Fine paintbrush

Blu-tack

ORDER OF WORK

Use the beading needle for attaching the beads, the no. 10 sharp needle when stitching with one strand of thread and the no. 8 when stitching with two strands.

Preparation

Silk fabric

Place the pellon onto the back of the silk print. Tack the two layers together around the edges.

Lace motif

Carefully cut away the background netting from around the lace motif, leaving approximately 1.5mm (1/16") to prevent the lace from fraying. Place the teabag into a small amount of hot water for several seconds. Using the fine paintbrush, dab hot tea onto the edges of the large lace flower's petals and onto some of the leaves. Dry the lace with a hairdryer, rinse in cool water and then dry again.

Using the photograph as a guide to placement, position the lace motif onto the right shoulder. Hold in place with stab stitches.

Thread embroidery

Lace motif

Work three detached chain leaves on the left hand side of the large lace flower. Using two thread colours, add 9 - 10 straight stitches for stamens, varying the lengths of the stitches from 5 - 10mm (1/4 - 3/8").

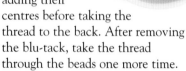

Outline one side of the curving stem and scrolls with stem stitch. Embroider tiny straight stitches within the large flower around the bases of the outer petals. Edge these petals with back stitch.

Dress

Outline the upper edge of the neckband with stem stitch. The lower edge will be embroidered after the band is beaded.

Using two strands of thread, stitch six wavy lines of varying lengths over the right shoulder.

Hat

Stitch across the lower edge of the brim with stem stitch and the olive thread. Change to the pink thread, and stitch across the upper edge in the same manner. Add several straight stitches just to the right of where the spray of flowers will be positioned.

Embroider the foliage above and below the brim with criss-crossing straight stitches to create fine feathery leaves. Add two pink detached chains on the right of the flower spray.

Bead embroidery

Lace motif

Add seven dark cream beads to the ends of the straight stitches for the stamens. Using the photograph as a guide to placement, attach the same colour beads along the stem on the

opposite side to the stem stitch. Include a section of eight rose pink beads on the lower half of the stem.

Scatter several dark cream beads around the smaller lace flower and outline the petal of the large lace flower near the top of the stem with yellow gold beads, as indicated in the photograph.

Dress

Attach two rows of olive green beads around the neckline. Below this work small white daisies using a yellow gold bead for each flower centre and five matte cream beads for the petals. Work the lower edge of the neckband with a row of stem stitch approximately 1cm (3/8") below the upper edge. Fill the remaining spaces within the neckband with dark grey-green beads.

Using tiny pieces of blu-tack on the back of each flower bead and using the photograph as a guide, position the flowers on the dress.

To secure the small pink flowers, bring the thread from the back to the front, through the bead and then to the back again. Lift the bead and remove the blu-tack. Pull the thread firmly to ensure the bead stays in position.

Repeat the procedure for the small white flowers and large flowers, adding their centres before taking the thread to the back. After removing the blu-tack, take the thread through the beads one more time.

Cover the red sections of the dress with silverlined crystal seed beads, attaching each one separately and leaving tiny spaces between the beads. Add rose pink and pale pink beads to the right shoulder and rose pink beads to the left shoulder and between the fingers of the gloved hand. Finish with a smattering of dark cream beads near the wrist of the gloved hand.

Hat

Position and attach the flowers in the same manner as those on the dress. Place the butterfly just off the edge of the hat. Add pale pink and olive green beads around the flowers for tiny buds.

Finally, individually attach dark grey-green beads near the ends of the brim as indicated in the photograph.

FINISHING

Place the finished embroidery face down on a well padded surface and press gently around the design. Take care not to press over the beaded areas.

COLOUR KEY

All thread embroidery is worked with one strand of thread unless otherwise specified. Use a single strand of thread for the beading.

Lace motif

Attaching lace = Q (stab stitch)

Large lace flower

Outer petals = W
(2 strands, straight stitch)

Outer petal outlines = W
(2 strands, back stitch), A

Stamens = V (2 strands, straight stitch), R (straight stitch), B

Leaves

Small leaves = V
(2 strands, detached chain)

Leaf outlines = W
(2 strands, back stitch)

Stem

Outline = R (stem stitch), B and F

Small spikes = W (2 strands, straight stitch)

Scattered beads = B

Dress

Neckband

Outline = V (stem stitch)

Upper edge = C

Flower petals = E

Flower centres = A

Foliage = D

Flowers on left shoulder

Large flower = I, K and L

Small pink flower = N

Flowers on right shoulder

Large flower = I, L and O

Small pink flowers = N

Flowers on right front

Large flower = I, L and O

Small pink flower = N

Small white flowers = I and L

Flowers on left front

Small pink flower = M

Small white flowers = I and L

Beads on dress = B, F, G and H

Wavy lines on right shoulder = V
(2 strands, stem stitch)

Hat

Brim

Lower outline = T (stem stitch)

Upper outline = U (stem stitch, straight stitch)

Main floral spray above brim

Very large flower = J and M

Large flowers = I, K and L

Small white flower = I and L

Tiny buds = C and H

Leaves = S (straight stitch),
U (detached chain)

Butterfly = P

Small spray below brim

Small pink flower = M

Tiny buds = C

Leaves = S (straight stitch)

Green beads = D

'HANAKO'S DREAM' BY JUDITH COOMBE,
INSPIRATIONS 47

- SUMMER'S JEWELS -

By Liz Vickery of South Australia

THIS DESIGN USES

Beading

REQUIREMENTS

Beads

Delica 11/0 glass beads

A = DBR211 opaque alabaster lustre

Maria George bugle beads 2.5mm (1/8″) long

B = 111 beige iris AB

Swarosvki rondelles 4mm (3/16″) wide

C = crystal x 120

Claw set diamantes 4mm (3/16″) wide

D = crystal x 19

Supplies

Beading thread

Beading needle

Background fabric

Embroidery hoop 25cm (10″) wide

ORDER OF WORK

Trace the design onto the right side of the background fabric using your chosen method. Mount the fabric in the hoop.

Stems and leaves

Bead the stems first, adding up to six beads at a time. Once a stem is complete, take the thread back through all the beads and pull firmly to help align them.

Stitch the leaves following the step-by-step instructions on page 61. Use six beads for the first row and four beads for the second row. Secure a bugle bead inside each leaf outline.

Flowers

Attach a diamante to the centre of one flower, taking the stitches through the two channels on the back. Bring the thread to the front near the centre to begin beading the petals.

Securing the beads by taking the thread through them twice, add a rondelle next to the centre and then one on the opposite side. Repeat this two more times so there are six petals.

Repeat for all remaining flowers.

FINISHING

Place the finished embroidery face down on a well padded surface and press gently around the design. Take care not to press over the beaded areas.

COLOUR KEY

Use a doubled strand of beading thread for the flowers and a single strand for all other beading.

Stems = A

Leaves

Outlines = A

Centres = B

Flowers

Centres = D

Petals = C

I QUESTION NOT IF THRUSHES SING,
IF ROSES LOAD THE AIR;
BEYOND MY HEART I NEED NOT REACH
WHEN ALL IS SUMMER THERE.
John Vance Cheney, Love's World

- GLORIOSA -

By Helan Pearce of Victoria

THIS DESIGN USES

Beading

REQUIREMENTS

Beads

Delica 11/0 glass beads

A = DBR671 satin olive

B = DBR672 satin off-white

C = DBR820 satin light pink

Pearl beads 6mm (1/4") wide

D = white x 2

Supplies

Beading thread

Beading needle

Background fabric

Piece of medium weight woven interfacing to fit background fabric

Felt for padding 10cm (4") square

Fusible appliqué paper 10cm (4") square

Water-soluble fabric marker

Embroidery hoop 20cm (8") wide

ORDER OF WORK

Trace the design onto the right side of the background fabric using your chosen method.

Trace the petal and leaf padding shapes onto the paper side of the appliqué paper. Fuse the appliqué paper to the felt and cut out the shapes. Remove the paper.

Place the interfacing onto the wrong side of the fabric and tack together around all sides.

Place the fabric in the hoop.

Flowers

Stitch the petals first. Beginning with the smallest piece of felt, attach three layers of felt, one on top of the other, with stab stitch. Cover the felt, following the step-by-step instructions on page 74. Repeat for all remaining petals. Lay a string of beads along the centre of each petal for the centre vein, working a small bead loop of 4 - 5 beads at the tip.

Attach a pearl bead to the centre of each flower. Surround each of these with five bead loops using nine beads for each loop.

Bud

Work the bud in the same manner as the flower petals, omitting the tip and centre vein. Stitch two rows of green beads at the base for the calyx.

Stems and scrolls

Following the step-by-step instructions on page 14, work the stems, attaching each bead separately. Stitch the scrolls in the same manner.

Leaves

Create the padded leaves in the same manner as the flower petals, omitting the centre vein and tip. Work the first two rows of each half with four beads, then one row of five beads, followed by four rows of four beads and then two rows of three beads. Except for the first and last rows, position an off-white bead at the outer edge of each row.

FINISHING

Place the finished embroidery face down on a well padded surface and press gently around the design. Take care not to press over the beaded areas.

COLOUR KEY

All stitching is worked using one strand of beading thread.

Flowers

Petals = B and C

Centre vein = A and B

Tip = A

Centre = A and D

Bud

Petal = C

Calyx = A

Stems = A

Leaves = A and B

Scrolls = B

- *Padded Beading* -

1. Trace the padding shapes onto the paper side of appliqué paper. Fuse the paper to the felt and carefully cut out each shape.

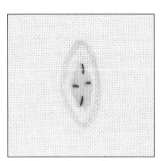

2. Centre the smallest piece inside the marked outline on the right side of the fabric. Secure with stab stitches.

3. Centre the medium sized padding shape over the first and secure as before. Repeat for the largest padding shape.

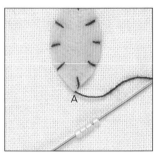

4. Bring the thread to the front at A, through the background fabric only at the base of the shape. Thread four beads onto the needle.

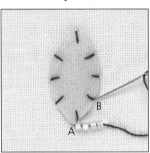

5. Take the needle to the back at B, going through the background fabric only.

6. Pull the thread through. Re-emerge through the felt approximately a bead's width away from A.

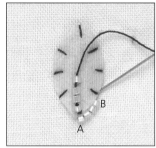

7. Thread four more beads onto the needle. Take the needle to the back a bead's width away from B, going through the background fabric only.

8. Pull the thread through. Attach one more group of four beads in the same manner.

9. Using the same method, work a row of five beads, then a row of six beads, followed by a row of five beads. Stitch two more rows of four beads.

10. Finish the first half of the shape with two rows of three beads.

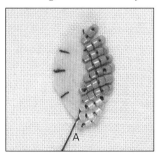

11. Return to the base of the shape and bring the thread to the front at A again.

12. Complete the second half of the shape as a mirror image of the first half. End off on the back of the fabric.

- SAMPLER -

By Liz Vickery of South Australia

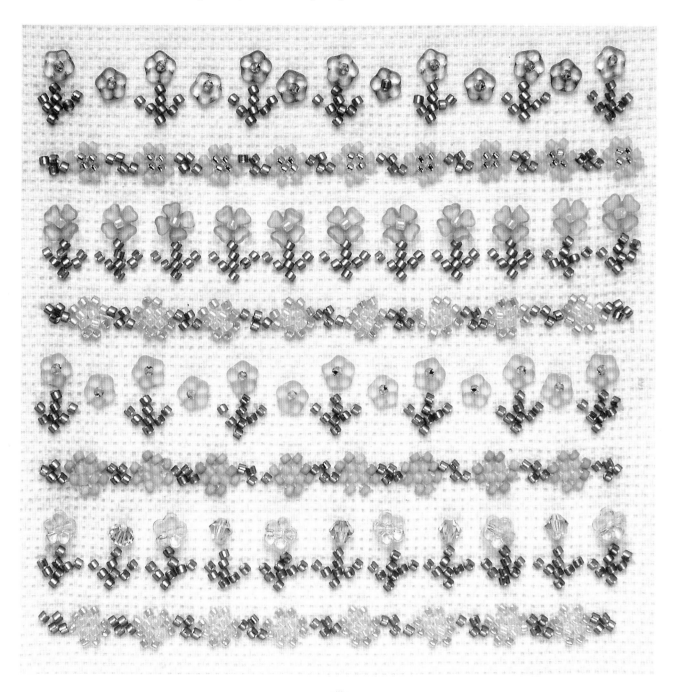

THIS DESIGN USES

Beading, Beadpoint

REQUIREMENTS

Beads

Delica 11/0 glass beads

A = DBR232 lined alabaster yellow

B = DBR257 lined alabaster blue

C = DBR356 matte lavender

D = DBR625 pearl light rose pink

E = DBR689 semi-matte silverlined light grey-green

F = DBR852 transparent matte light topaz AB

Maria George 15/0 Ceylon beads

G = 4112 gold

Czech glass rondelles 4mm (3/16″) wide

H = light rose x 5

Flower beads 6mm (1/4″) wide

I = matte yellow x 13

J = matte tanzanite x 13

K = pink x 6

L = blue x 11

Supplies

Beading thread

No. 10 straw (milliner's) needle

16 count Aida cloth

Embroidery hoop 20cm (8″) wide

ORDER OF WORK

Work a line of tacking down the centre of the fabric. Mount the fabric in the hoop.

Row 1

Beginning with the middle flower and following the chart, stitch the stem and leaves using beadpoint. Work the remaining stems and leaves in the same manner. Attach the flowers following the instructions on page 27.

Row 2

Following the chart for placement, stitch the flowers and leaves across the row using beadpoint.

Row 3

Stitch the stems and leaves in the same manner as those in row 1, following the chart for placement. Attach the flowers in the same manner as before.

Row 4

Using different bead colours and starting with a leaf, work this row in a similar manner to row 2.

Row 5

Work in exactly the same manner as row 1, but use matte yellow flowers instead of tanzanite ones.

Row 6

Using different colours, repeat row 4.

Row 7

Work the stems and leaves in exactly the same manner as row 3. Alternating between a pink flower and a pink rondelle, attach these to the tops of the stems.

Row 8

Using different colours, repeat row 4.

FINISHING

Place the finished embroidery face down on a well padded surface and press gently around the design.

COLOUR KEY

All stitching is worked using a double strand of beading thread.

Row 1

Flower petals = J

Flower centres = G

Stems and leaves = E

Row 2

Flower petals = F

Flower centres = G

Leaves = E

Row 3

Flower petals = L

Flower centres = A

Stems and leaves = E

Row 4

Flower petals = D

Flower centres = A

Leaves = E

Row 5

Flower petals = I

Flower centres = G

Stems and leaves = E

Row 6

Flower petals = C

Flower centres = F

Leaves = E

Row 7

Large flowers = K

Small flowers = H

Stems and leaves = E

Row 8

Flower petals = B

Flower centres = A

Leaves = E

CENTRE

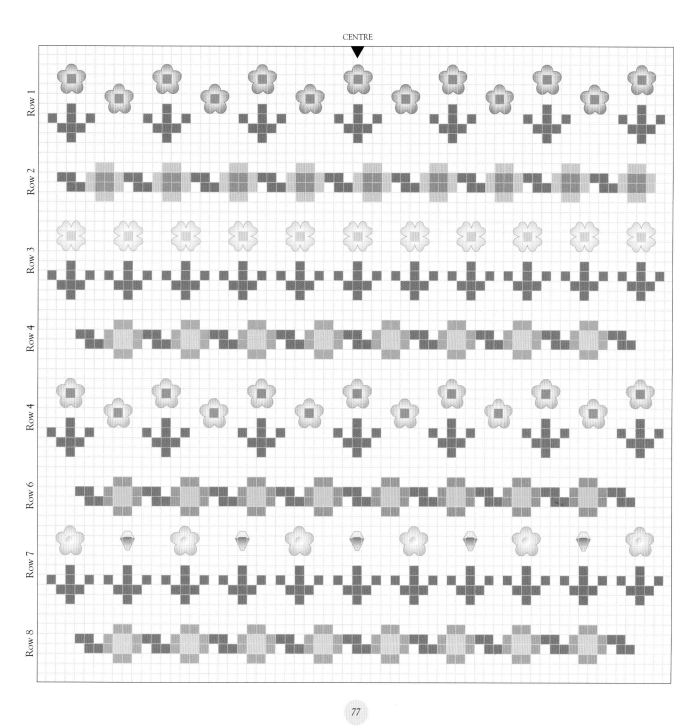

Row 1

Row 2

Row 3

Row 4

Row 4

Row 6

Row 7

Row 8

- TWILIGHT'S BREATH -

By Jane Davis of USA

REQUIREMENTS

Beads

11/0 glass seed beads

A = purple/blue

B = pink/gold

15/0 glass seed beads

C = very light pink

D = light pink

E = light crimson

F = dark crimson

G = dark navy

H = metallic gold

I = matte pale mustard

J = matte olive

K = lime green

L = dark green

M = greenlined topaz

Flower beads 5mm (3/16") wide

N = light blue x 3

Drops 4mm (3/16") long

O = transparent pink/crystal AB x 4

Supplies

Beading thread

Beading needles

Background fabric

Embroidery hoop 15cm (6") wide

THIS DESIGN USES

Beading

ORDER OF WORK

Trace the design onto the right side of the background fabric using your chosen method. Mount the fabric in the hoop.

Rose

Using the back stitch method and adding three beads at a time, stitch the stems and centre veins of the leaves. Outline the leaves in the same manner. Fill the leaves with rows of beads, using lazy squaw stitch and mixing the bead colours to give a mottled appearance.

Bead the sepals with back stitch and then outline the petals. Fill the petals using the same method.

Stock

Stitch a line of the darkest green beads for the stem. Following the step-by-step instructions on page 26, work a circle of five beads for each flower. Add a single pink/gold bead to each centre.

Bead the flat leaves following the step-by-step instructions on page 61. Use 5 - 7 beads for the first side and 3 - 5 for the second side. Fill each one with a single bead.

To work the freestanding leaves, bring the thread to the front of the fabric at the base of the leaf. Thread five beads onto the needle and slide them down to the fabric. Take the needle back through the last two beads, thread a further three beads onto the needle and then take it to the back of the fabric. Work a further fourteen leaves in the same manner.

Attach the drops so they nestle among the foliage.

Forget-me-nots

Stitch the stems in the same manner as the rose stems and the leaves in the same manner as the flat stock leaves, using five beads for the first side and three beads for the second side. Attach the flower beads with a navy seed bead. Work a cluster of five beads for each bud.

FINISHING

Place the finished embroidery face down on a well padded surface and press gently around the design. Take care not to press over the beaded areas.

COLOUR KEY

All stitching is worked using one strand of thread.

Rose
Stems = K and L
Leaves
Outlines = H, I, J, K, L and M
Veins = K
Filling = H, I, J, K, L and M
Flower
Petals = C, D, E, F and G
Sepals = H, I, J, K, L and M

Stock
Stem = M
Leaves
Flat leaves = H, I, J, K, L and M
Raised leaves = H, J, K, L and M
Flowers
Petals = A
Centres = B
Buds = O

Forget-me-nots
Stems = H, J, K, L and M
Leaves = H, I, J, K and L
Flowers = G and N
Buds = G and H

- PAPILLON -

By Helen Eriksson of South Australia

THIS DESIGN USES

Beading, Couching, French knot
Long and short stitch, Stem stitch
Straight stitch

REQUIREMENTS

Beads

Delica 11/0 glass beads

A = DBR31 metallic bright gold

B = DBR158 opaque lavender AB

C = DBR380 matte metallic green/pink

Diamante flower beads
6mm (¹/₄") wide

D = silverlined crystal x 2

Swarovski rondelles 3mm (¹/₈") wide

E = light amethyst x 6

F = amethyst x 10

Czech fire polished beads
4mm (³/₁₆") wide

G = French rose AB x 36

Embroidery threads

H = gold metallic cord 25cm (10")

I = gold fine metallic thread

Supplies

Beading thread

Beading needle

No. 8 crewel needle

No. 16 chenille needle

Lace butterfly motif

Piece of silk for lining butterfly

Background fabric

Embroidery hoop 15cm (6") wide

ORDER OF WORK

Use the beading needle for attaching the beads, the chenille needle for working with the gold cord and the crewel needle for all remaining embroidery.

Use the photograph as a guide to bead and colour placement.

Butterfly

Tack the lace butterfly to the right side of the piece of silk fabric and treat them as one piece. Place the fabric in the hoop.

Body

Following the step-by-step instructions on page 21 and starting at the top of the body, stitch rows of beads across the width. Add more beads as the body gets wider and decrease the number of beads at the tail.

Wings, tail and antennae

Using the fine gold thread, embroider the scrolls on the wings with stem stitch. Keep the stitches tiny to give the scrolls a rounded appearance. Work a French knot at the centre of each scroll.

After completing the scrolls, work the base of the tail between the lower wings, in long and short stitch.

Stitch the antennae next, bringing the gold cord to the front at the top of the body just above the first bead. Using beading thread, couch the cord in place at approximately 2 - 3mm (¹/₈") intervals. Take the gold cord through to the back at the end of the curl on the antennae and

secure on the back of the fabric with tiny overcast stitches. Work the remaining half of the antennae in the same manner.

Using the tiny lavender beads, attach them over the scroll markings on the inner wings. Add a light mauve rondelle to the centre of each scroll.

Following the step-by-step instructions on page 82, work a crystal flower in each of the scallops on the upper wings. Work a diamante flower at the lower end of each wing, follow-ing the step-by-step instructions on page 83.

COLOUR KEY

All embroidery is worked with one strand of thread.

Butterfly

Body = C

Wings and tail

Gold scrolls = I (stem stitch French knot, 2 wraps)

Tail = I (long and short stitch)

Centres of crystal flower markings = F

Petals of crystal flower markings = G

Diamante flower markings = A and D

Beaded scrolls = B

Wing outlines = B

Antennae = H and I (straight stitch, couching)

Attaching the butterfly to the background fabric

Remove the silk fabric and lace from the hoop and carefully trim away the excess silk from around the butterfly.

Add some fray stopper to the edge of the silk to prevent it from fraying.

Position the butterfly onto the background fabric. Using the lavender beads, stitch them in place around the shape of the butterfly and the division between the upper and lower part of each wing. Attach the beads individually and just inside the outer edge of the lace.

FINISHING

Place the finished embroidery face down on a well padded surface and press gently around the design. Take care not to press over the beaded areas.

- *Crystal Flower* -

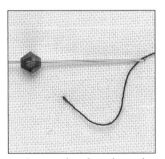

1. Secure the thread on the back of the fabric and bring it to the front for the centre. Thread a single rondelle onto the needle.

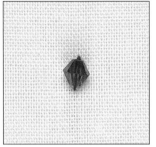

2. Slide the rondelle down the thread to the fabric and attach using the back stitch method.

3. Bring the thread to the front close to the centre. Thread a crystal onto the needle.

4. Slide the crystal down the thread to the fabric and attach using the back stitch method.

5. Bring the thread to the front at the inner end of the opposite flower petal.

6. Attach a second crystal in the same manner as before.

7. Attach a second pair of crystals in the same manner as the first pair.

8. Repeat the process one more time to complete the petals. Six crystals are attached.

- *Diamante Flower* -

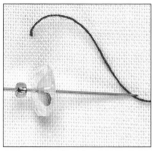

1. Secure the thread on the back of the fabric and bring it to the front for the centre of the flower. Thread a flower bead and then a small glass bead onto the needle.

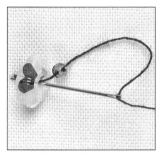

2. Slide the beads down the thread to the fabric. Take the needle back through the flower bead only.

3. Pull the thread through. Work 1 - 2 tiny back stitches behind the flower to secure.

4. Bring the thread to the front just beyond the edge of the flower bead.

5. Thread a small glass bead onto the needle and attach with a back stitch. Ensure the hole of the bead faces the flower bead.

6. Continue attaching small glass beads individually, around the edge of the flower bead, in the same manner. End off on the back of the fabric.

Properties of Crystals

Angelite *dispels anger and negativity*

Aquamarine *enhances your ability to think quickly*

Green Aventurine *enhances leadership qualities*

Harlequin quartz *provides vitality*

Fire agate *dispels fear*

Citrine *is a healing stone and it helps you feel cheerful and lighthearted*

Chrysocolla *eases emotional heartache and stress*

Emerald *enhances memory and aids domestic bliss*

Jade *brings peace and tranquillity, it promotes long life and protects you from accidents*

Moonstone *provides protection while travelling*

Rose quartz *is excellent for emotional healing and finding love*

Zircon *promotes physical, emotional, spiritual and mental unity*

- SHIMMER -

By Liz Vickery of South Australia

THIS DESIGN USES

Beading

REQUIREMENTS

Beads

Delica 11/0 glass beads

A = DBR689 semi-matte silverlined light grey-green

11/0 glass seed beads

B = pink

C = crystal AB

14/0 glass seed beads

D = crystal AB

Swarovski flower beads 6mm (1/4") wide

E = fuchsia x 15

Sequins 6mm (1/4") wide

F = crystal AB

Supplies

Beading thread

Beading needle

Background fabric

Embroidery hoop 20cm (8") wide

ORDER OF WORK

Trace the design onto the right side of the background fabric using your chosen method. Mount the fabric in the hoop.

Stems and leaves

Adding 3 - 4 beads at a time, work the stems and leaf outlines using the back stitch method. Within each leaf, add a row of overlapping sequins following the instructions on page 31.

Flowers

Outline the petals in the same manner as the leaves. Stitch a single pink seed bead at the centre of one flower. Surround this centre bead with a circle of six beads. Attach five flower beads in a circle around the previous circle of beads. Attach each one following the instructions on page 27. Fill the petals with scattered sequins, attaching each one with a small seed bead. Work the remaining two flowers in the same manner.

FINISHING

Place the finished embroidery face down on a well padded surface and press gently around the design. Take care not to press over the beaded areas.

COLOUR KEY

All stitching is worked using one strand of beading thread.

Flowers

Centre = B, C and E

Petal outlines = B

Petals = D and F

Stems = A

Leaves

Outlines = A

Veins = F

Glass beads

Beads have been made of glass for over 5,000 years. The discovery of fire was the essential step in glass bead making. The Egyptians used a method known as 'core-forming' where they would hold pieces of glass over a flame. As the glass gradually softened, it was wrapped around a metal mandrel which resulted in the formation of particularly intricate ornaments. These early beads, or vessels, have been found in numerous burial tombs.

Even today, many beads are made by holding glass rods over a flame then gently winding the molten glass over mandrels.

- RAINBOW WHORLS -

By Heather Sterling of South Australia

THIS DESIGN USES

Beading

REQUIREMENTS

Beads

Delica 11/0 hex cut glass beads

A = DBC24 metallic green

B = DBC25 metallic blue iris

Delica 11/0 glass beads

C = DBR12 metallic raspberry

Supplies

Beading thread

Beading needle

No. 9 crewel needle

Background fabric

Embroidery frame 38cm (15") square

ORDER OF WORK

Trace the design onto the right side of the background fabric using your chosen method. Mount the fabric in the frame.

Use the crewel needle for couching the spirals of beads and the beading needle for threading and attaching the remaining beads.

Full spirals

Using separate spools of thread, string the blue iris and green beads. There is no need to cut the threads at this stage.

Starting just inside the marked line of one circle, take the end of one string of beads to the back of the fabric and secure. Position the string of beads so the edge of the beads butts the marked outline. Using a different thread, couch between each bead. Continue spiralling and couching between the beads until reaching the centre.

Stitch all remaining spirals in the same manner, ensuring that the edge of one spiral just touches the edges of the adjacent ones.

Partial spirals

Starting and finishing on the edge of the design, couch beads around the outer edge of one partial circle. Turn the fabric and couch the second row alongside the first row. Continue working rows back and forth until the circle is filled. Repeat for the remaining partial spirals.

Background

Using the back stitch method, scatter raspberry beads in the spaces between the spirals.

COLOUR KEY

All stitching is worked using one strand of thread.

Complete spirals = A and B

Partial spirals = B

Background = C

Zodiac Stones

Aries	Red jasper
	Cornelian
Taurus	Rose quartz
	Orange cornelian
Gemini	Citrine, Tiger's eye
Cancer	Aventurine
	Chrysoprase
Leo	Rock crystal
	Golden quartz
Virgo	Citrine
	Yellow agate
Libra	Orange citrine
	Smoky quartz
Scorpio	Deep red cornelian
Sagittarius	Chalcedony
	Blue quartz
Capricorn	Onyx, Cat's eye
Aquarius	Dark blue turquoise, Tiger's eye
Pisces	Amethyst

Edgings
& Fringes

- CLEOPATRA -

By Jane Davis of USA

REQUIREMENTS

Beads

11/0 glass seed beads

A = greenlined topaz

Mill Hill petite glass beads

B = 42024 heather mauve

C = 42031 citron

Drops 6mm (1/4") wide

D = bottle green AB

Czech fire polished oval beads 4mm (3/16") long

E = green

Dagger beads 10mm (3/8") long

F = copper

Flower beads 5mm (3/16") wide

G = green

Spacer beads 4mm (3/16") wide

H = green

Supplies

Beading thread

Beading needle

Gimp braid or base fabric

ORDER OF WORK

Secure the thread on the wrong side of the fabric and bring it to the front at your starting position on the left hand side.

1. First row. Thread A x 3 onto the needle. Take the needle to the back of the fabric approx one bead's width away from where it emerged.

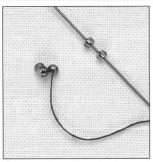

2. Bring the needle to the front and take it through the last bead. Thread on A x 2.

3. Take the needle to the back of the fabric approximately one bead's width away from where it emerged.

4. Repeat steps 2 and 3 across the fabric for the desired distance.

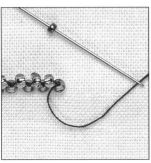

5. Second row. Working from right to left, take the needle through the last bead (A). Thread a B onto the needle.

6. Take the needle through the second to last green bead and then thread another B onto the needle. Add four more B beads in the same manner.

7. Take the needle through the next A and then thread on B, A, B. Take the needle back through the A of the previous row.

8. Pull the thread through to form a picot.

9. Continue across the row, adding B beads between those of the previous row and working a picot every five beads.

10. Third row. Bring the thread to the front alongside the right hand end of the A bead below the last picot. Take the needle through the A bead to the right.

11. First scallop. Thread beads in the following order: C x 2, A, F, A, F, A, F, A, C x 2.

12. Take the needle through the A bead just to the left of the next picot.

13. Pull the thread through. Take it through the A bead at the base of the picot and the A bead just to the right.

14. Second scallop. Thread beads in the following order: C x 3, A, D, A, C x 4. Take the needle through the A beads below the picot in the same manner as before.

15. Third scallop. Work the scallop as a mirror image of the previous one.

16. Continue repeating the pattern of three scallops across the row.

17. First drop. Using a new thread, bring it to the front through the A bead at the right hand end of the second scallop.

18. Take the needle through the last C bead of the scallop and thread beads in the following order: C, A, E, B x 3.

19. Take the needle back through E, A, C x 2 and A x 3 directly below the picot. Pull the thread through.

20. Second drop. Thread beads in the following order: C, A, C x 3, H, G, B x 3.

21. Take the needle back through G, H, C x 3, A. Thread a C onto the needle.

22. Pull the thread through. Take the needle, from left to right, through A x 3 directly below the picot.

23. Pull the thread through. **Third drop.** Work in the same manner as the first drop.

24. Repeat the three drops below every third picot.

- BOREALIS -
By Jane Davis of USA

REQUIREMENTS

Beads

6/0 glass beads

A = rose pink AB

8/0 glass seed beads

B = matte green/purple

11/0 glass seed beads

C = rose pink AB

Delica 8/0 glass beads

D = DBL5 medium blue iris

Bugle beads 5mm (3/16″) long

E = rose pink AB

Drops 6mm (1/4″) long

F = crystal AB

Czech fire polished oval beads 4mm (3/16″) long

G = peacock AB

Leaf beads 12mm (1/2″) long

H = pink AB

Flat flower beads 5mm (3/16″) wide

I = blue-green

Supplies

Beading thread

Beading needle

Gimp braid or base fabric

ORDER OF WORK

Secure the thread on the wrong side of the fabric and bring it to the front at your starting position on the left hand side.

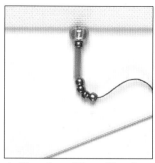

1. First drop. Thread beads in the following order: A, C, E, and C x 4.

2. Take the needle back through the first seed bead of the group of four.

3. Pull the thread through. Thread on E, C, and A.

4. Take the needle through the fabric 8mm (5/16") away from the first bead. Pick up a tiny portion at the fold.

5. Pull the thread through. **Second drop.** Take the needle back through A.

6. Pull the thread through. Thread beads in the following order: C, E, C, B, I, C x 2, F, C x 2.

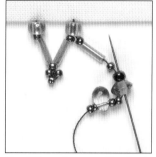

7. Take the needle back through I and B.

8. Thread on C, E, C, and A. Take the needle through the fabric as before.

9. Third drop. Take the needle back through A and then thread on C, E, C, B, D, B, G, I, C x 3, H, C x 3.

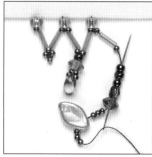

10. Take the needle back through I, G, B, D and B.

11. Pull the thread through. Thread on C, E, C, and A. Take the needle through the fabric as before.

12. Repeat the second drop and then the first drop. Continue working drops to form a zigzag pattern.

- PEARL -

By Jane Davis of USA

Overlapping loops are used to create this design.

REQUIREMENTS

Beads

11/0 glass seed beads

A = pearl

8/0 glass beads

B = pearl

C = gold AB

Pearl beads 4mm (³/16") wide

D = ivory

Pearl beads 6mm (¹/4") wide

E = ivory

Supplies

Beading thread

Beading needle

Gimp braid or base fabric

ORDER OF WORK

Secure the thread on the wrong side of the fabric and bring it to the front at your starting position on the left hand side.

1. First loop. Thread beads in the following order: B, A x 3, C, A x 3.

2. Take the needle back through C and thread on A x 3, and B. Pull the thread through.

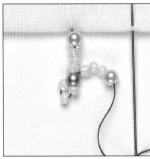

3. Take the needle through the fabric approximately 12mm (¹/2") from the beginning of the loop. Pick up a tiny portion at the fold.

4. Pull the thread through. **Second loop.** Take the needle through the last bead.

5. Pull the thread through. Thread beads in the following order: A x 5, C, D, C, A x 5, and B.

6. Take the needle through the fabric approximately 12mm (1/2") from the beginning of the loop. Re-emerge through the fold, halfway between the two ends of the last loop.

7. Pull the thread through.

8. Third loop. Form a loop in exactly the same manner as the second loop.

9. Flip the third loop out of the way. **Fourth loop.** Take the thread back through the fabric and the last bead of the second loop.

10. Pull the thread through. Thread beads in the following order: A x 7, B, C, B, C, E, C, B, C, B, A x 7, and B.

11. Flip the third loop down. Take the needle through the fabric approx 6mm (1/4") from the end of the previous loop. Re-emerge through the last bead of the third loop.

12. Pull the thread through.

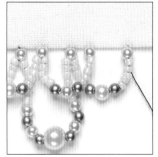

13. Fifth loop. Work a loop in the same manner as the second loop. Re-emerge through the last bead of the fourth loop.

14. Flip the fifth loop out of the way.

15. Sixth loop. Work a sixth loop in the same manner as the second loop.

16. Repeat the pattern of six loops across the fabric.

- ALICE'S GARDEN -

By Jane Davis of USA

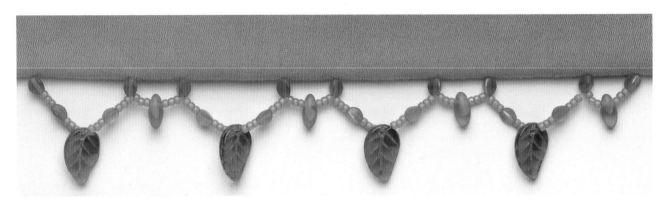

REQUIREMENTS

Beads

11/0 glass seed beads

A = matte aqua

Dagger beads 8mm (5/16") long

B = frosted blue-green

Triangle niblet beads 5mm (3/16") long

C = frosted blue-green

Leaf beads 13mm (1/2") long

D = blue-green

Supplies

Beading thread

Beading needle

Gimp braid or base fabric

ORDER OF WORK

Secure the thread on the wrong side of the fabric and bring it to the front at your starting position on the left hand side.

1. First scallop. Thread beads in the following order: C, A x 3, C, A x 3, D, A x 3, C, A x 3, C.

2. Take the needle through the fabric 25mm (1") from the beginning of the scallop. Pick up a tiny portion at the fold.

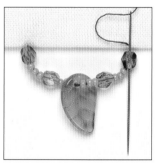

3. Pull the thread through. **Second scallop.** Take the needle through the last bead.

4. Pull the thread through. Thread beads in the following order: A x 3, B, A x 3, C.

5. Take the needle through the fabric 12mm (1/2") from the beginning of the scallop. Pick up a tiny portion at the fold.

6. Pull the thread through. Repeat the pattern of large and small scallops across the fabric.

Zulu Beadwork - the meaning of colours

In Zulu tradition, young girls learned beadwork and the symbolic use of colours from their older sisters. The patterns and colours would show whether a woman was engaged, married, unmarried, had children or unmarried sisters, what region she was from and what her social standing was.

The basic geometric shape was the triangle and it was used with a maximum of seven colours. These colours are black, blue, yellow, green, pink, red and white. Each colour has two meanings, one positive, one negative, except white. White has only one meaning, purity and spiritual love.

	POSITIVE	NEGATIVE
Black	marriage, rebirth	death, sadness
Blue	faithfulness, request	hostility, dislike
Yellow	wealth, garden	badness, thirst, withering
Green	contentment	discord, illness
Pink	promise, high status	poverty, laziness
Red	love, strong emotion	anger, heartache
White	Spiritual love, purity	

- BLUE LOTUS -

By Jane Davis of USA

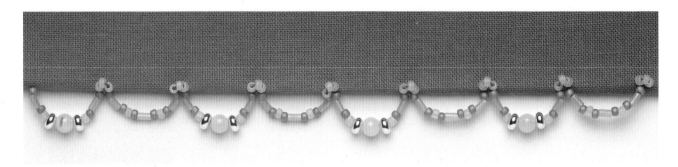

Alternating scallops and picots form a dainty edging.

REQUIREMENTS

Beads

11/0 glass seed beads

A = frosted ice blue

B = frosted antique blue

Bugle beads 3mm (¹/8″) long

C = frosted ice blue

Round agate beads 5mm (³/16″) wide

D = milky white

Spacer beads 4mm (³/16″) wide

E = silver

Supplies

Beading thread

Beading needle

Gimp braid or base fabric

ORDER OF WORK

Secure the thread on the wrong side of the fabric and bring it to the front at your starting position on the left hand side.

The Lotus

To the ancient Egyptians, a lotus bud or sesen was a symbol of rebirth. It closes in the evening and falls to the water; in the morning it opens and is lifted above the surface. Its behaviour emulates that of the sun. Because of this rising and setting, it is also a symbol of death and rebirth. According to one creation myth, a giant lotus emerged from the watery chaos at the beginning of time. Out of its centre, the sun itself rose on the first morning.

1. First scallop. Thread beads in the following order: B, C, B, A, E, D, E, A, B, C, B.

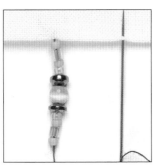

2. Take the needle, from back to front, through the fabric approximately 15mm (⅝") from the first bead. Pick up a tiny portion at the fold.

3. Pull the thread through. **Picot.** Thread on A x 3.

4. Take the needle, from front to back, through the fabric a bead's width from where it emerged.

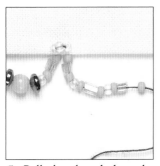

5. Pull the thread through. **Second scallop.** Thread beads in the following order: B, C, B, A, B, C, B, A, B, C, B.

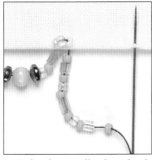

6. Take the needle, from back to front, through the fabric approximately 15mm (⅝") from the beginning of the scallop. Pick up a tiny portion at the fold.

7. Pull the thread through. **Picot.** Work a second picot in the same manner as the first one.

8. Repeat the pattern across the fabric.

Pearls

No-one knows the earliest people to collect and wear pearls but they have had a place in history for thousands of years.

India's sacred books and epic tales are filled with references to pearls. In one Hindu legend, the god Krishna discovers pearls when he plucks the first one from the sea and presents it to his daughter Pandaïa on her wedding day.

China's long recorded history also provides ample evidence of the importance of pearls and in Egypt, decorative mother-of-pearl was used at least as far back as 4200 BC. During the first century BC, Roman women upholstered couches with pearls and sewed so many into their gowns that they actually walked on their pearl-encrusted hems.

- LASIANDRA -

By Jane Davis of USA

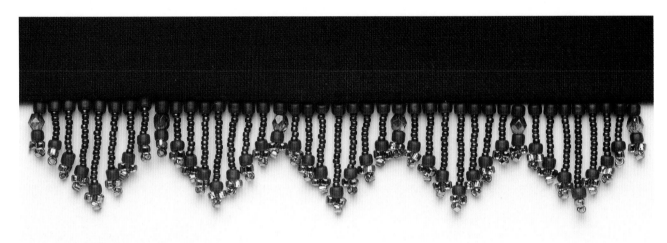

REQUIREMENTS

Beads

15/0 glass seed beads

A = indigo AB

11/0 glass seed beads

B = silverlined mauve AB

8/0 glass beads

C = matte purple

Czech fire polished beads
4mm (3/16″) wide

D = amethyst AB

Supplies

Beading thread

Beading needle

Gimp braid or base fabric

ORDER OF WORK

Secure the thread on the wrong side of the fabric and bring it to the front at your starting position on the left hand side.

1. First drop. Thread beads in the following order: C, D C, and B x 3.

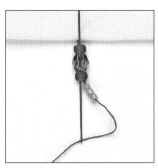

2. Take the needle back through C, D, C.

3. Take the needle through the fabric, re-emerging a bead's width away.

4. Pull the thread through.

5. Second drop. Thread beads in the following order: C, A x 6, C, B x 3.

6. Take the needle back through C, A x 6, C and then the fabric, re-emerging a bead's width away.

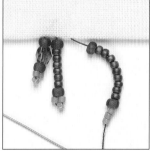

7. Pull the thread through. **Third drop.** Thread beads in the following order: C, A x 9, C, B x 3.

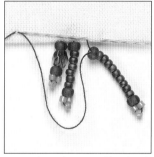

8. Take the needle back through C, A x 9, C and then the fabric, re-emerging a bead's width away.

9. Fourth and fifth drops. Form these in the same manner as the previous drop but use A x 12 for the fourth drop and A x 15 for the fifth drop.

10. Repeat the fourth, then third and second drops to complete one pattern repeat.

11. Repeat the pattern across the fabric.

- IRISH MOSS -

By Jane Davis of USA

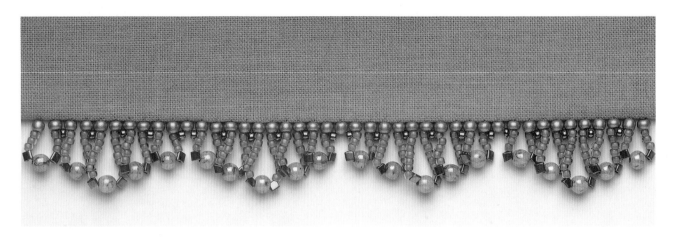

REQUIREMENTS

Beads

8/0 glass seed beads

A = matte gold

11/0 glass seed beads

B = bronze

C = lime green

8/0 triangle beads

D = brass

Round agate beads 5mm (3/16″) wide

E = light green/brown

Supplies

Beading thread

Beading needle

Gimp braid or base fabric

ORDER OF WORK

Secure the thread on the wrong side of the fabric and bring it to the front at your starting position on the left hand side.

Seed beads

Seed beads are also known as 'Conterie'.

They are produced from hollow glass tubes that are chopped and then refired for smoothness and colour. The beads are sold by weight or in prestrung hanks.

Japan, Italy and the Czech Republic are among the leading producers of seed beads.

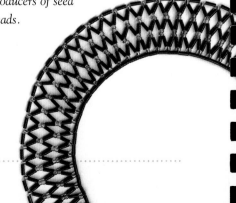

1. First loop. Thread beads in the following order: A, C x 3, D, E, D, C x 3, A.

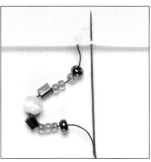

2. Take the needle through the fabric next to the first bead, picking up a tiny portion at the fold.

3. Pull the thread through. **Picot.** Take the needle through the last bead and thread on B, A.

4. Pull the thread through. Take the needle through the fabric, picking up a tiny portion at the fold.

5. Pull the thread through. **Second loop.** Take the needle back through the last bead.

6. Pull the thread through. Thread beads in the following order: C x 5, D, E, D, C x 5, A.

7. Complete the loop and work a picot as before.

8. Work a third loop in the same manner, using C x 7, D, E, D, C x 7, A.

9. Working picots in between, repeat the second loop then the first loop.

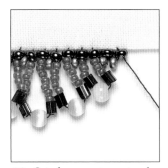

10. Stitch two picots in the same manner as before.

11. Repeat the pattern across the fabric.

CELADON, INSPIRATIONS 42

- NIGHTSHADE -

By Jane Davis of USA

REQUIREMENTS

Beads

11/0 glass seed beads

A = frosted royal blue

15/0 glass seed beads

B = peacock AB

Dagger beads 10mm (3/8″) long

C = royal blue

Supplies

Beading thread

Beading needle

Gimp braid or base fabric

ORDER OF WORK

Secure the thread on the wrong side of the fabric and bring it to the front at your starting position on the left hand side.

Nightshade (belladonna)

The name belladonna originates from the historic use by ladies (Bella Donna is Italian for beautiful lady) to dilate their pupils; an extract of belladonna was used as eye drops as part of their makeup preparations.

According to practitioners of witchcraft, nightshade is ruled by Hecate and can turn into an old hag on Walpurgis Night, or April 30. It is also used in flying ointments. Of the twelve recipes for flying ointments, six call for deadly nightshade.

Optometrists and ophthalmologists use belladonna to this day for pupil dilation in eye examinations, though the dose is extremely small.

1. First scallop. Thread beads in the following order: B x 5, A, C, A, C, A, C, A, B x 5.

2. Take the needle through the fabric approximately 15mm (⁵/₈") from the beginning of the scallop. Pick up a tiny portion at the fold.

3. Pull the thread through. **First picot.** Take the needle through the last bead and thread on B x 2.

4. Take the needle through the fabric, picking up a tiny portion at the fold.

5. Pull the thread through. **Second picot.** Take the needle through the last bead and thread on A x 3, B.

6. Take the needle through the fabric, picking up a tiny portion at the fold.

7. Pull the thread through. **Third picot.** Work in the same manner as the first picot.

8. Repeat the pattern across the fabric.

The healing power of crystals

Amber	**Aventurine**	**Blue apatite**	**Goldstone**	**Hematite**	**Selenite**	**Serpentine**	**Topaz**
helps your body heal itself and lessens depression and stress	is good for skin diseases and improving the complexion	curbs the appetite and is known as the dieter's stone	helps strengthen bones and fight arthritic pain	aids sleep and relieves headaches	aids in aligning the skeletal system and promotes muscle flexibility	eliminates parasitic infestations within your body	balances the nervous system and is good for overcoming exhaustion and mood swings

- MILLEFIORI -

By Jane Davis of USA

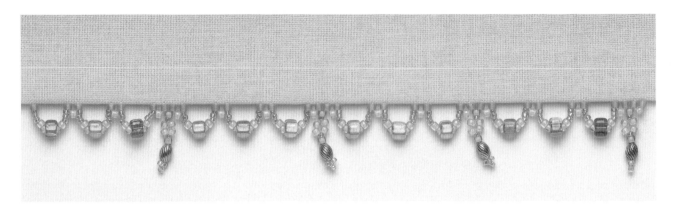

REQUIREMENTS

Beads

11/0 glass seed beads

A = yellow

B = frosted green

15/0 glass seed beads

C = baby blue

5/0 triangle beads

D = amber

Oval metal beads 5mm (³/16″) long

E = copper

Supplies

Beading thread

Beading needle

Gimp braid or base fabric

ORDER OF WORK

Secure the thread on the wrong side of the fabric and bring it to the front at your starting position on the left hand side.

Millefiori beads

Millefiori means a thousand flowers in Italian. In Venice, where they have been made since the 15th century, they are also known as mosaic beads.

The making of a Millefiore bead involves two different craftsmen. Glass canes are made in a glass factory. The slices or chips of these canes are called murrine, and these are sold to the bead maker who places the chips onto a wound glass core.

From about 1800 to 1950, tubular glass millefiore beads were made for the African Bead Trade. The Ashante call these mosaic beads 'Chachasao'.

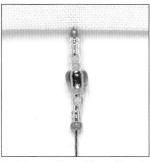

1. First scallop. Thread beads in the following order: B, C x 3, A x 2, D, A x 2, C x 3, and B.

2. Take the needle through the fabric approximately 8mm ($5/16$") from the beginning of the scallop. Pick up a tiny portion at the fold.

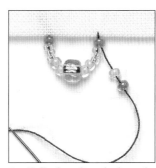

3. Pull the thread through. **First picot.** Take the needle through the last bead and thread on A, B.

4. Take the needle through the fabric, picking up a tiny portion at the fold. Pull the thread through.

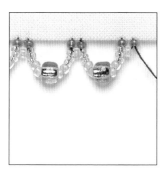

5. Work two more scallops and picots in the same manner.

6. Drop. Take the needle through the last bead and thread beads in the following order: A, C, A x 2, C, B, E, and C x 3.

7. Take the needle back through E, A, C.

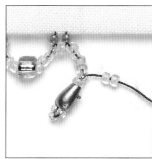

8. Pull the thread through. Thread on A x 2.

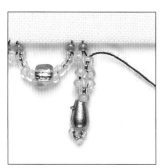

9. Take the needle through C, A. Pull the thread through.

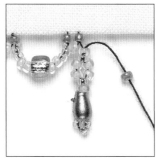

10. Thread on B.

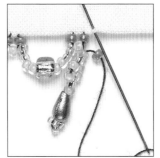

11. Take the needle through the fabric as before.

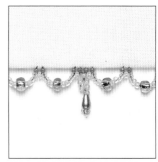

12. Work a picot and continue the pattern across the fabric.

- KILLARNEY -

By Jane Davis of USA

REQUIREMENTS

Beads

11/0 glass seed beads

A = matte teal

B = satin bronze AB

Pressed glass rondelles
5mm (³/₁₆″) wide

C = green and gold

Bugle beads 3mm (¹/₈″) long

D = bronze AB

Gemstone chips

E = pale amber

Supplies

Beading thread

Beading needle

Gimp braid or base fabric

ORDER OF WORK

Secure the thread on the wrong side of the fabric and bring it to the front at your starting position on the left hand side.

Beaded bags

The first bags made entirely of beads appeared in the seventeenth century. They were really small coin purses. The eighteenth century was a time of opulence, particularly in the French Court. Beaded bags were a popular accessory. During the reign of Napoleon, reticules were essential fashion accessories for ladies.

The professional French beadworkers produced bead embroidery with super fine beads known as sable. The beads completely covered the purse and were so minute that there were as many as 1,000 beads per square inch (25mm).

1. First scallop. Thread beads in the following order: A x 5, C, A x 5.

2. Take the needle through the fabric approximately 12mm (1/2") from the beginning of the scallop. Pick up a tiny portion at the fold.

3. Pull the thread through. **First drop.** Take the needle through the last bead and thread on A x 3, D, B, C, and B x 3.

4. Take the needle back through all these beads except for the last three.

5. Pull the thread through. Thread an A onto the needle, then take the needle through the fabric. Pick up a tiny portion at the fold.

6. Pull the thread through. **Second drop.** Work this in the same manner as the first drop except thread A x 7 instead of A x 3.

7. Third drop. Work in the same manner as the first drop.

8. Second scallop. Work in the same manner as the first scallop.

9. Third scallop. Thread beads in the following order: B x 3, E, B x 2, E, B x 2, E, B x 3, A.

10. Take the needle through the fabric approximately 15mm (5/8") from the beginning of the scallop. Pick up a tiny portion at the fold. Pull the thread through.

11. Repeat the pattern across the fabric.

- BAROQUE -

By Liz Vickery of South Australia

Stringing beads

REQUIREMENTS

Beads

Maria George 11/0 glass beads

A = 6113 brown iris

Delica 11/0 glass beads

B = DBR602 silverlined garnet

C = DBC501 gold iris

Bugle beads 3mm (1/8") long

D = gold

*Czech fire polished beads
4mm (3/16") wide*

E = garnet

*Czech fire polished drops
10mm x 6mm wide (3/8" x 1/4")*

F = garnet

Swarovski rondelles 4mm (3/16") wide

G = Dorado

Bead caps 4mm (3/16") wide

H = gold

Supplies

Beading thread

Beading needle

Gimp braid or base fabric

Clear craft glue

ORDER OF WORK

Apply a small amount of craft glue along the entire length of the braid on the wrong side. This helps to prevent the loops of the braid from sagging under the weight of the beads.

Using a 1m (39 1/2") length of beading thread, secure it to the wrong side of the braid at your starting position. Eight bead drops make up one repeat of the design.

Beginning at the top of the first bead drop, thread the beads onto the needle in the order indicated on the diagram.

After threading on the last bead, take the needle back through all the beads except for the last one and pull the thread through. Take the thread through the loop of the braid and secure but do not cut. Carry the thread to the position for the second bead drop. Following the diagram, thread these beads in the same manner as the first drop. Secure the thread as before.

Continue stringing bead drops until the desired number are worked.

1	2	3	4	5	6	7	8
A	A	A	A	A	A	A	A
C	C	C	C	C	C	C	C
A	A	A	A	A	A	A	A
Bx9	Bx9	Bx9	Bx9	Bx9	Bx9	Bx9	Bx9
A	A	A	A	A	A	A	A
C	C	C	C	C	C	C	C
A	A	A	A	A	A	A	A
D	D	D	D	D	D	D	D
A	C	C	C	C	C	C	C
C	D	D	D	D	D	D	D
A	A	C	C	C	C	C	A
G	C	D	D	D	D	D	C
A	A	A	C	C	C	A	A
H	G	C	D	D	D	C	G
E	A	A	A	C	A	A	A
H	H	G	C	D	C	G	H
A	E	A	A	A	A	A	E
G	H	H	G	C	G	H	H
A	A	E	A	A	A	E	A
C	G	H	H	G	H	H	G
Ax12	A	A	E	A	E	A	A
C	C	G	H	H	H	G	C
A	Ax12	A	A	E	A	A	Ax12
G	C	C	G	H	G	C	C
A	A	Ax12	A	A	A	Ax12	A
H	G	C	C	G	C	C	G
E	A	A	Ax12	A	Ax12	A	A
H	H	G	C	C	C	G	H
A	E	A	A	Ax12	A	A	E
H	H	H	G	C	G	H	H
F	A	E	A	A	A	E	A
A	H	H	H	G	H	H	H
	F	A	E	A	E	A	F
	A	H	H	H	H	H	A
		F	A	E	A	F	
		A	H	H	H	A	
			F	A	F		
			A	H	A		
				F			
				A			

- WATER'S EDGE -

By Liz Vickery of South Australia

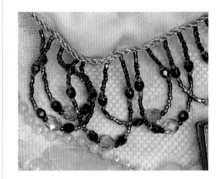

THIS DESIGN USES

Attaching a bead to the end of a bead
Stringing beads

REQUIREMENTS

Beads

Maria George 11/0 glass beads

A = 6113 brown iris

Delica 11/0 glass beads

B = DBR323 matte metallic purple iris

C = DBR373 matte metallic under leaf green

D = DBR799 dyed opaque matte dark lavender

E = DBR857 transparent matte light

F = DBR865 matte dark chocolate AB

Czech fire polished beads 4mm (³/16″) wide

G = French rose AB

Czech fire polished beads 6mm (¹/4″) wide

H = light amethyst

Swarovski rondelles 4mm (³/16″) wide

I = dark amethyst

J = erinite

K = dark tanzanite

Swarovski rondelles 6mm (¹/4″) wide

L = light tanzanite

Bead caps 4mm (³/16″) wide

M = silver

Supplies

Beading thread

Beading needle

Gimp braid or base fabric

Clear craft glue

ORDER OF WORK

Apply a small amount of craft glue along the entire length of the braid on the wrong side. This helps to prevent the loops of the braid from sagging under the weight of the beads.

Using a 1m (39 ¹/2″) length of beading thread, secure it to the wrong side of the braid at your starting position. Each bead drop is worked in exactly the same manner.

Beginning at the top of the first bead drop, thread the beads onto the needle in the following order: A, D, A, E x 8, A, D, A, I, A, D, A, F x 10, A, D, A, G, A, D, A, C x 12, A, D, A, K, A, D, A, B x 14, A, D, A, J, A, M, L, M, A, M, H, A.

After threading on the last bead, take the needle back through all the beads except for the last one and pull the thread through. Take the thread through the loop of the braid and secure but do not cut. Carry the thread to the position for the second bead drop. Continue stringing bead drops in the same manner until the desired number are worked.

Making fringes

Always check you have enough thread to complete a drop before starting it.

If your drop has a kink in it, you may have missed taking the thread through a bead.

If your drop will not pull up evenly, you may have taken the needle through the beading thread at some point. Unthread the needle and take the thread back to the last bead added.

When starting and finishing a thread, leave a 9cm (3 ¹/2″) tail. When the fringe is complete, pass this thread back down the nearest drop and trim the excess.

The
Patterns

MAGNOLIA
See pages 52 - 55
Actual size

PANDORA'S GARDEN
See pages 40 - 42
Actual size

1

2

3

4

5

115

JAPONICA
See pages 43 - 45
Actual size

TOP

TWILIGHT'S BREATH
See pages 78 - 79
Actual size

STARFLOWER
See page 39
Actual size

DRAGONFLY
See pages 56 - 58
Actual size

MARIE
ANTOINETTE
See pages 50 - 51
Actual size

PUNICA
See pages 62 - 63
Actual size

VICTORIANA
See pages 46 - 47
Actual size

PAPILLON
See pages 80 - 83
Actual size

PADDING TEMPLATES

GLORIOSA
See pages 72 - 74
Actual size

SIAM
See pages 48 - 49
Actual size

SHIMMER
See pages 84 - 85
Actual size

RAINBOW WHORLS
See pages 86 - 87
Actual size

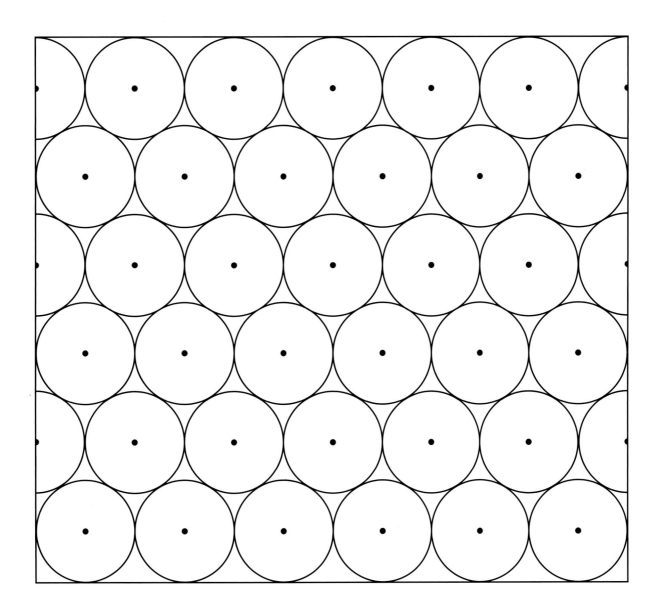

Note:
Coloured type denotes step-by-step instructions
Bold type denotes section
Italic type denotes designer

NEEDLEWORK BOOKS FROM COUNTRY BUMPKIN

Filled with beautiful projects, easy instructions, superb photography and full size patterns.

Inspirations Baby

Inspirations Bridal

Inspirations Gifts

The World's Most Beautiful
Embroidered Blankets

Embroidered Christening Gowns

Embroidered Bags & Purses

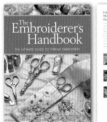
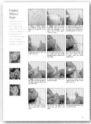

The Embroiderer's Handbook

The Embroidered Village Bag

The Embroidered Patchwork Bear

QUARTERLY MAGAZINES

Each magazine features stunning projects, magnificent photography, clear step-by-step instructions and full size patterns.

Inspirations

Australian Smocking & Embroidery

OTHER TITLES IN THE A-Z SERIES

Over 2,000,000 copies sold.

A-Z of Embroidery Stitches

A-Z of Embroidered Flowers

A-Z of Stumpwork

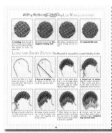

Detailed, clear step-by-step instructions

A-Z of Bullions

A-Z of Ribbon Embroidery

A-Z of Quilting

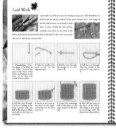 

Stunning original designs

A-Z of Smocking

A-Z of Sewing for Smockers

A-Z of Needlepoint

FOR MORE INFORMATION
ON ANY TITLE, OR TO PLACE
AN ORDER, CONTACT
COUNTRY BUMPKIN:

Phone 08 8372 7600

Fax 08 8372 7601

Email
mailorder@countrybumpkin.com.au

Website
www.countrybumpkin.com.au

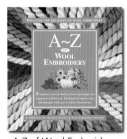

A-Z of Wool Embroidery

A-Z of Crewel Embroidery

A-Z of Thread Painting

We sincerely thank the wonderful designers who have so readily shared their designs.

Judith Coombe, page 66

Jane Davis, pages 78, 89, 92, 94, 96, 98, 100, 102, 104, 106 and 108

Helen Eriksson, page 80

Helan Pearce, pages 50, 56 and 72

Anna Scott, pages 43 and 62

Heather Sterling, page 86

Karen Torrisi, page 39

Liz Vickery, pages 40, 46, 48, 52, 59, 64, 70, 75, 84, 110 and 112

Inside front cover PEARLS OF WISDOM by Dana Cox, Inspirations issue 5

Page 5 THE DRAGONFLY by Jane Nicholas, Inspirations issue 41

Page 13 WATERMARK by Jane Nicholas, Inspirations issue 17

Page 38 ELIZABETHAN DRAGONFLIES by Jane Nicholas, Inspirations issue 32

Page 88 RARE VINTAGE by Liz Vickery, Inspirations issue 47

Page 114 DAMSELFLY by Jane Nicholas, Inspirations issue 29

Inside back cover ANTIQUE GOLD by Liz Vickery, Inspirations issue 31